Hogs on 66

Hogs on 66

Best Feed and Hangouts for Road Trips on Route 66

Michael Wallis
Marian Clark

Council Oak Books

San Francisco / Tulsa

Council Oak Books, Tulsa, Oklahoma 74104
©2004 by Michael Wallis and Marian Clark. All rights reserved
Published 2004

09 08 07 06 05 04   6 5 4 3 2 1

Portions of this book appeared in a slightly altered form in *Main Street of America Cookbook* © 1997 by Marian Clark and *The Route 66 Cookbook* © 1993 by Marian Clark

A portion of the Introduction text previously appeared in an article written by Michael Wallis in the January-February 1999 issue of *Oklahoma Today*.

Cover design by Idea Studios, Tulsa

Interior design by Margaret Copeland

Grateful acknowledgments are made to the following people for use in this book of the photographs on the pages indicated:

Collection of Reba McClanahan, Myers-Duren Harley-Davidson, Tulsa, front cover historical photos, 31, 51, 58, 69, 91, 110, 125, 133, 171

Collection of Matthias Guenther 1, 4 (left), 7 (right), 9, 10, 11 (both), 12, 17, 23, 24, 27 (right), 28 (right), 32, 33, 39, 41, 43, 46, 48, 54, 55, 56, 57 (right), 63, 67 (top), 70 (left), 73, 78 (both), 81, 82, 85, 91, 92 (right top and bottom), 93, 95 (top), 97, 103, 108, 113, 114 (right top), 115 (left bottom), 122 (right and left), 123, 124 (top and bottom), 126, 136 (right), 138, 142, 145, 148, 149 (both), 152, 153, 155, 157, 158, 159, 164, 166, 169

Collection of Michael and Suzanne Wallis 25, 62, 66 (bottom right), 79, 84, 90, 95 (bottom), 99, 117, 156, 173

Dan McNeil 87

"Milwaukee" Harry Jaeger 6, 7 (left), 13, 20, 28 (left), 29, 35, 40, 42, 44, 53 (left), 65, 70 (right), 71, 72, 92 (left), 94, 101, 114 (left), 118, 119, 134, 136 (left), 141, 144, 150, 170

Heidi and Ken Creasman 16, 36, 37, 52, 53 (right), 66 (left and top right), 68, 75, 76, 98 (right), 114 (right bottom), 130, 154, 183

Ken Clark 14

Linda Scott 21, 49, 111, 115 (left top), 137, 160, 162, 179

Marian Clark 4 (right), 5, 18 (both), 26, 27 (left), 64

Marilyn Pritchard 181

Suzanne Wallis vii, 3, 15, 34, 57 (left), 112, 115 (right), 129, 139, 140, 147, 161

Terry Allen 120, 121

Trond Moberg 59, 60, 67 (bottom), 98 (left), 107

Collection of Bob Lile 100

Mary Simon 176

Jean Dennison 109, Authors' photo, back cover

Printed in Canada

For Suzanne, my true love and riding companion through life
— MICHAEL WALLIS

To my biker husband Ken, my best and most loyal supporter,
and to Megan, Andrew, Brad and Haley, who will continue our mystical journey.
— MARIAN CLARK

Contents

Road Warrior Kent Meacham

Acknowledgments

MY SINCERE AND EVERLASTING THANKS to my friend Zigy Kaluzny, who not only taught me how to ride a motorcycle properly and safely, but who also shared with me his abiding love for open road bike travel.

Thanks to my dear wife, Suzanne, friend and lover and the person whose own love for motorcycles proved contagious and claimed me.

Much appreciation goes to my coauthor Marian Clark, the incomparable culinary maestro of the Mother Road and to the good folks at Council Oak Books, especially Sally Dennison and Ja-Lene Clark.

A salute of gratitude to James Fitzgerald, Jr., who serves me very well as a literary agent and whose close friendship I value more than he knows.

As always, I offer my gratitude to Cosmo, our charming feline muse. And finally, a huge thanks goes to all the many men and women I have had the honor of riding with on America's Main Street and beyond.   — MICHAEL WALLIS

THE IDEA OF JOINING TWO OF AMERICA'S MOST FAMOUS ICONS, Route 66 and Harley-Davidson, came from the creative team at Council Oak Books. When Michael and I met with Sally Dennison and Ja-Lene Clark, their enthusiasm was contagious. We talked about possibilities, divided assignments, and began to work. The challenge was to incorporate favorite foods with the fun and freedom of the road, Harley-Davidson style. Michael's rich reservoir of stories and practical travel guides quickly merged with biker-friendly recipes and suggestions on where to stop and what to see.

Many of the recipes for *Hogs on 66* were collected as I searched Route 66 for *The Main Street of America Cookbook* (Council Oak Books, 1997). A handful came from *The Route 66 Cookbook* (Council Oak Books, 1993). I will always be indebted to the individuals who contributed to both of those books. Harley-Davidson dealers, bikers both here and abroad, and many new friends along Route 66 shared the remaining recipes and their own stories.

Ann Arwood tested scores of recipes from my earlier cookbooks. Mary Gubser continues to inspire like no other, Michael and Suzanne Wallis have been a guiding forces since we first met in 1990. Council Oak published my first cookbook in 1993. The staff continues to believe in this effort and support Route 66 projects. My biker husband, Ken, has been my best and most loyal supporter. You are all great!

I included dishes that we felt would be especially biker-friendly and added some of the best from regional fare. Glaida Funk, Kathleen Miller, Lynn Bagdon, Fran Eikhoff, Tonya Pike, Scott Nelson, Laurel Kane, Maria Rinaldi, Joann Harwell, Lori Kassner, Ken Turmel, Karen Harrill, Ananda Shorey and countless others contributed, answered questions, shared, material and reminded me of what a wonderful road family we share.

Trond Moberg, Harley-Davidson travel guide extraordinaire, shared wisdom from his notebooks as well as several favorite recipes from Norway. Matthias Guenther, Kleinmachnow, Germany, provided photographs and memories from his Harley trip with Christina Hey in the fall of 2003. My sincere thanks. This project has been so much fun!   — MARIAN CLARK

Introduction
Ride to Live, Live to Ride

"It's not the destination, it's the journey." — HARLEY-DAVIDSON SAYING

Route 66 and motorcycles are a natural, especially if the biker is on a Harley-Davidson. Two major American cultural icons, Route 66 and Harley go together like a sizzling burger and a slab of cheddar cheese, like hot apple pie and strong coffee, like smoked ribs and spicy sauce. They make a heady combination as potent and memorable as a fiery pot of chili.

The Mother Road and cycles have always represented the romance of traveling the open road. Harley-Davidson, founded in 1903, and Route 66, created in 1926, enjoyed a sweet courtship that soon blossomed into a full-blown love affair. The marriage of the two American treasures is solid. The honeymoon is endless.

The chemistry between Harley and Route 66 stems from the fact that both of these revered institutions celebrate freedom and a spirit of unity. That independence and a commitment to tradition can prove intoxicating whenever a biker saddles up and cruises Route 66 — a road that promises motion, excitement, adventure, and always delivers.

To better understand the strong bond between Harley and America's Main Street, picture this scene way out west on a stretch of concrete two-lane Route 66, stained from the vermilion earth of surrounding wheat fields.

A man clad in supple leathers and faded denim slips outside and welcomes the morning. Faint tracks of night stars whither and vanish and a hint of breeze stirs the weeds along a wire fence. Filled with stout coffee and plenty of courage, the man sees in a heartbeat that it is a postcard-perfect day — tailor-made for a ramble on a motorcycle. A smile buds on his lips. All is right with the world.

Mindful that a motorcycle is not just another vehicle but a distinct lifestyle, the man considers himself doubly blessed. For he will not be riding just *any* cycle — he owns a Harley. This fellow is a true believer. He fears no evil, lives life full bore, and holds to the opinion that on the eighth day God created Harley-Davidson.

Leather skullcap, gauntlets, and goggles in place, the man secures the straps on the saddlebags, swings a booted leg over the seat, and mounts his gleaming machine — a Heritage Softail Classic. Just a turn of the ignition key, a push on the starter button, a gentle twist of the throttle, and the brawny Harley engine rumbles to life.

As he glides off in the direction of his dreams, the rider experiences what many others can only fantasize. The process of unfettered travel takes over. All thoughts disappear of the kid's college tuition, a volatile stock market, and the favorite football team's losing season. Every one of his senses is heightened and at full alert. For the next several hours, man and machine blend into a sweet concoction and dance through time and space.

Convinced that life truly does begin on the off-ramp, the biker sticks to the old road. No need for maps, turnpike change, or reservations. The possibility of pure adventure waits around every curve and bend. The ride is all that matters. Time becomes meaningless. Only the aroma of succulent ribs wafting from a roadside pit reminds the rider to pause for a late lunch.

The road beckons. With each passing mile, the man astride the metal-and-chrome pony is transformed into a Chisholm Trail drover, an escaping desperado, a Kiowa scout. He becomes a young Brando, the Lone Ranger, *Easy Rider* incarnate. He is nineteen once again, en route to a Jimi Hendrix concert. Images of Jack Kerouac and Ken Kesey dance in his head.

Through sunshine and buffeting wind and beneath the shadows and light of heaven, the rider cruises the Mother Road all day long. Bound only by his imagination, he does not turn the bike around and head for home until long after the moon rises.

Wherever the bike goes, heads turn. Everyone hears it coming. Nothing else sounds like a Harley. World-class writers have recounted the din of combat, timber crashing to the ground, a newborn infant's cry, the laughter of a woman in love, but not one of them has even come close to describing the distinctive purr, growl, and roar of a Harley-Davidson motorcycle.

Ironically, at one time the Harley engine earned the nickname "Silent Gray Fellow," in deference to the standard model's quiet muffler and stock shade of gray, the color of choice except for the optional basic black. But that was in 1907 when the Harley-Davidson Motor Company was still in its infancy.

Since those early years, Harley — just like Route 66 — has endured good and bad times while evolving into a cherished national icon. Of course, much of that air of reverence which developed around the Harley name comes from the fact that Harley-Davidson is the sole remaining motorcycle manufacturer in the United States and the nation's number-one seller of heavyweight bikes. The Harley is as American as Will Rogers, hamburgers, and the bald eagle, which proudly serves as the company symbol. The Harley is also much more, at least in the minds and imaginations of all those who choose to ride one.

As a 1998 cover story about Harley-Davidson in *Popular Mechanics* put it, the Harley cycle is "a poke in the eye to mainstream sensibilities, a rolling sculpture, a club, a support group, a fantasy, a noisy declaration of independence, a way of life, a brotherhood, a religion, an obsession, something to believe in, an escape, and probably the best consumer marketing device in history."

When it comes to the so-called Harley mystique, perhaps the words emblazoned across a popular biker T-shirt say it best: "If I have to explain, then you wouldn't understand."

Yet hundreds of thousands of Harley owners — men and women from around the world and virtually every walk of life — need no explanation. They get the message loud and clear. Ranging from factory workers to brain surgeons, these brothers and sisters of the road hold their Harleys in high esteem and consider themselves members of a very special family.

And that is why the Harley family of riders is so attached to Route 66. Many bikers consider the Mother Road prime riding territory — nothing short of Hog heaven on earth.

I also know this because on two occasions my wife, Suzanne Fitzgerald Wallis, and I led hundreds of Harley riders — representing almost every state in the union and more than a dozen foreign nations — down the entire length of Route 66. Harley Owners Group, better known as H.O.G., sponsored both tours. The first tour took place in 1995 and the second in 2001, to mark the 75th anniversary of Route 66.

These treks were documented by national and international media and are considered landmark events in the annals of Harley and Route 66 history. Both of the historic journeys are forever tattooed in our memories.

Like every journey we make, the two Harley tours of the Mother Road were filled with magical moments. We saw so much along the way and we paid our respects at the old and new businesses that continue to mushroom along the old road. Some of the stories that were gathered on those journeys are included in this book.

As the title implies, *Hogs on 66: Best Feed and Hangouts for Roadtrips on Route 66* provides an assortment of yarns, practical advice, useful tips, and an array of colorful photographs to enhance the biker experience on the Mother Road. Beyond that the book will also serve as a useful resource and tool for anyone traveling Route 66, even those who prefer four wheels or more for their journey.

Included in the book is plenty of the wisdom of my friend and co-author, Marian Clark. The recognized authority on all culinary aspects of Route 66, Marian shares generous tips on biker havens as well as provides hospitality and dining options along the highway. She also offers up heaping spoonfuls of biker recipes for some of the tastiest road chow on the old highway.

All together we believe it is a savory stick-to-the-ribs stew sure to please any open road traveler.

Enjoy the ride and be sure to save room for pie.

— MICHAEL WALLIS

Illinois

Fast Facts from Illinois

- Approximate Route 66 mileage in Illinois — 280

- "Historic Route 66" signs are brown and white in Illinois.

- Current official Illinois highway maps include Route 66.

- Illinois Route 66 preservationists have completed more projects than those of any other state.

- Illinois is home to the only maple grove along Route 66.

Illinois Biker Road Rules

- Safety helmet, not required

- Eye Protection, required

Where to buy stuff

- FUNK'S GROVE — All-American Maple "Sirup." Be sure to spell sirup the Funk's Grove way.

- BROADWELL — Ernie Edwards' Pig-Hip Restaurant Museum. "The Old Coot" will be glad to spin a yarn for you.

- STAUNTON — Henry's Old Route 66 Emporium and Rabbit Ranch. Meet Montana or her kids — or her grandkids.

Must see in Illinois

- CHICAGO — Navy Pier on the shores of Lake Michigan

- CICERO — Sportsman's Park Race Track and Hawthorne Racecourse

- JOLIET — The Empress Casino and Harrah's Joliet Casino

- LEXINGTON — 1926 "Memory Lane" 66 alignment just north of town; stop to admire the restored billboards right out of our past.

- MCLEAN — Dixie Truckers Home, under new management but currently home to the Illinois Route 66 Hall of Fame

- SPRINGFIELD — Bill Shea's Gas Station Museum; a great collection of gas station memorabilia and old Harley-Davidson signs

Where the Road Begins

Chicago ⊙

66

ILLINOIS

Springfield ★

- *MOUNT OLIVE* — Soulsby Station, the road's oldest gas station

- *COLLINSVILLE* — 70 foot catsup bottle atop a 100 foot tower, a restored tribute to Brooks Catsup

- *CHAIN OF ROCKS BRIDGE* — Get off your bike, stretch, and take a walk on the longest pedestrian bridge in the world

Favorite hangouts for food and drink

- *CHICAGO*
THE BERGHOFF, 17 W. Adams Street
  Authentic Chicago since 1890, holder of the 1st liquor license in Chicago after prohibition

BILLY GOAT TAVERN, Kinzie and Michigan Avenue

LOU MITCHELL'S, Jackson and Canal

INDIAN HEAD PARK: WOLF'S HEAD INN, 6937 Joliet Road

- *WILLOWBROOK*
DELL RHEA CHICKEN BASKET, 645 Joliet Road

- *JOLIET*
THE OLD KEG RESTAURANT AND PUB, 20 West Jackson

- *WILMINGTON*
LAUNCHING PAD DRIVE-IN, Route 53

- *BRAIDWOOD*
POLK-A-DOT DRIVE-IN, Route 53

- *GARDNER* — RIVIERA RESTAURANT, 1 mile north of Gardner, 5650 Route 53

- *DWIGHT* — FEDDERSON'S PIZZA, Old city 66

- *PONTIAC* — OLD LOG CABIN, Pontiac Road and North Aurora

- *SPRINGFIELD*
  - COZY DOG DRIVE-IN, 2935 S. 6th Street
  - DUDE'S SALOON, 1900 Peoria, where the bikers gather

- *FARMERSVILLE* — ART'S RESTAURANT, I-55 at Exit 72

- *LITCHFIELD* — ARISTON CAFE, Route 66 at IL 16

- *HAMEL* — EARNIE'S, IL 157 and IL 140

Zen of the Mother Road

— MICHAEL WALLIS

It was a day I'll never forget. A balmy summer Sabbath morning and I'm on my Heritage Softail at the head of a procession of hundreds of other Harleys ridden by riders from around the world. My true love and life partner, Suzanne, is on my bike right behind me and I can feel her excitement as she wraps her arms around my waist and kisses my shoulder.

The chance of a lifetime — to lead a Harley parade on America's Main Street in "The City of Big Shoulders" and I got the call. Not bad for a 60's-vintage former Marine sergeant. Now, we're talking enough bikers to form at least a couple or maybe three battalions. They hail from forty-four states and a dozen foreign nations. The oldest rider is 82 and the youngest is just four years old.

Although Route 66 is a two-way highway running east and west, most Road Warriors worth their grit prefer starting in Chicago and then striking out along 2,448 miles to the bluffs in Santa Monica overlooking the roaring Pacific.

We are going all the way down Route 66 — from Chicago, through eight states and three time zones. To start the journey off right, hundreds of us on our bikes will cruise in a long procession from our gathering place well south of Chicago and go to the heart of the city where Route 66 both begins and ends.

Bikers where the road begins

After 45 minutes we approach our destination. The start of Route 66, originally at Jackson Boulevard and Michigan Avenue, has moved a few times as various streets became one-way for traffic. Now the old route officially begins at Adams Street and Michigan Avenue, near the Art Institute of Chicago guarded by a pair of bronze lions. An historic Route 66 sign marking the official end of Route 66 stands at Jackson and Michigan and a sign declaring the start of the Mother Road welcomes travelers at Adams and Michigan.

The biker parade moves into Chicago's Loop — the crossroads of the country — beneath the shadow of the Sears Tower, one the tallest buildings in the world. As we glide across Michigan Avenue we glance to our right and there before us in Grant Park is a sea of yellow.

Engines are roaring in chorus and then the signal is given. Off we go with an escort of motorcycle cops who switch off with their counterparts as we move into different jurisdictions. Fortunately, since it is early Sunday, there is little traffic. We also discover that someone has some pull with Cook County and the City of Chicago. Rolling down the expressways we spy snowplows and trucks conveniently blocking the on-ramps. This morning Harley owns the road.

Before long the distinctive downtown skyline comes into view. I glance in my mirror and snaking behind me — as far as the eye can see — are nothing but shining motorcycles.

Sears Tower on the Mother Road

7

There is little time to take it all in but we finally figure out that this is a group of people in flowing gauzy yellow robes and they are meditating. They also are completely and utterly silent in stark contrast to the roaring and rumbling motorcycles passing them in review. The sound of hundreds of engines bounces and reverberates off the canyon of buildings yet not one of the yellow figures so much as twitches or shows any sign that they are aware of us.

Minutes later, after we all park our bikes in long rows and pose for countless photographs, we learn that the men and women in the park were Buddhists at prayer. When I finally get back to the site where they had congregated I find the Buddhists have gone. I wonder if I had really seen them after all or if they were an urban mirage. Suzanne assures me they were real, as do other bikers who also were struck by their presence.

There will be no return procession. The parade is over. Everyone is on their own for the rest of the day, free to check out points of interest on Jackson and Adams or prowl other parts of the city. Groups of bikers head straight to Lou Mitchell's, a favorite eating establishment for Route 66ers. Others go to the Art Institute or gather for more photos beneath the Route 66 signs.

We have a few cups of coffee before we climb on our scooter and take our leave.

The rest of that day and all the rest of that memorable journey across America, my thoughts went back to the moment when we flashed past the yellow robed Buddhists in Grant Park. I recalled that Buddhists believe in the concept of rebirth. With that in mind, I thought it appropriate that we had come upon the Buddhists in Chicago at the beginning and the end of a highway that has constantly experienced rebirth and rejuvenation.

I also considered that central to the Buddhist path to nirvana, or enlightenment, is the understanding and acceptance of impermanence. Everyone passes on. Nothing lasts forever. That gives life its newness and surprise.

Maybe that was what Robert Pirsig was telling us when he wrote *Zen and the Art of Motorcycle Maintenance*. The book is more than the details behind a cross-country motorcycle journey taken by a man and his eleven-year-old son. It is also the man's quest for truth and understanding.

That is exactly what we encountered on that memorable Harley tour along the Mother Road. It is what we still find every time we make the trip. For those fleeting moments in time — through rain and searing sun and across mountains and deserts — we are on our own pilgrimage of self-discovery and renewal. ■

Recipes from Illinois
— MARIAN CLARK

JUICY SLABS OF MEAT LOAF, slathered with aromatic tomato sauce, rank right up there at the top for satisfying biker victuals. This version came directly from a new cookbook, *We Work for Food*, published by the Route 66 Association of Illinois Preservation Committee. The group, headed by John and Lenore Weiss, has provided hands-on help to save barns, gas stations, diners, bridges, and signs all along Route 66 in this state "where Route 66 begins."

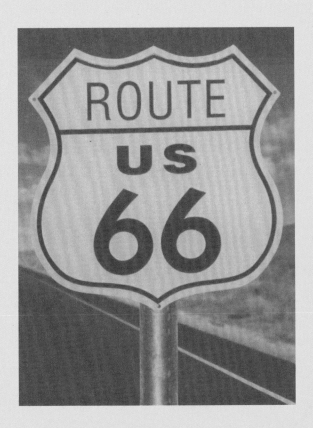

Judy's World Famous Meat Loaf
The Official Route-66-of-Illinois Favorite Recipe
JUDY SCHWALLENSTECKER

Sauce:
½ cup catsup
1½ teaspoons mustard
½ teaspoon ground nutmeg
⅓ cup brown sugar
2 tablespoons cider vinegar

Meat Loaf:
2 pounds lean ground beef
1 cup crushed cornflakes
½ teaspoon black pepper
2 teaspoons salt
1 medium onion, chopped
2 eggs
2 tablespoons minced parsley

Mix sauce ingredients and heat for a few minutes. Stir cornflakes into ground beef. Add remaining ingredients and ⅔ of the heated sauce. Shape into one large or two smaller loaves. Place in a 9x11 baking dish. Bake in a preheated 375-degree oven for 45 minutes. Spread remaining sauce over the top and continue baking for 15 minutes. Allow to stand for 10 minutes before slicing. 8 servings.

BIKERS ARE ALWAYS WELCOME when Chicago's Greek community celebrates each August at the Greek Town Festival held on Halstead Street between Monroe and

Van Buren. Food and drink comes from over fifteen Greek restaurants whose chefs prepare a wide array of traditional food. Entertainment includes dancing, ancestral and contemporary Greek music, fortune-telling, and spectacular food.

Keftethes
Greek Meatballs

1 pound ground beef
2 eggs
3 slices dry bread, crumbled
1 onion, finely shopped
3 tablespoons dry mint, crumbled
1 teaspoon salt
¼ teaspoon pepper
Flour for coating
Oil for frying

Mix the ingredients well. The mixture should be soft. With wet hands, roll into cocktail-sized meatballs, using about 1 level tablespoon of the mixture for each. Roll each lightly in flour and deep fry for 2-3 minutes.

   Instead of frying, these may be baked in the oven at 325 degrees for about 5 minutes, then turned and baked 5 more minutes. Approximately 36 meatballs.

FOR SOUP AS ALL-AMERICAN AS WILL ROGERS, try this hearty blend. It was originally included in *First There Must Be Food*, a fund-raising cookbook published by the Volunteer Service Department at Chicago's Northwestern Memorial Hospital.

The El, Chicago

Beef and Lentil Soup
First There Must be Food

3 tablespoons all-purpose flour
2 teaspoons salt
¼ teaspoon pepper
2 pounds beef for stewing, cut into ½ inch cubes
3 tablespoons vegetable oil
5-6 cups water
5 medium carrots, scraped and thinly sliced
2 cups sliced celery
2 large onions, chopped
1 cup dried lentils, washed and sorted
1 tablespoon lemon juice
1½ teaspoons salt
1 teaspoon dried whole thyme

Combine flour, 2 teaspoons salt, and pepper in a medium bowl; dredge beef in flour mixture.

   Heat oil in a large Dutch oven. Add beef and cook until browned on all sides. Add water; cover and simmer 45 minutes. Skim off any fat. Stir in carrot, celery, onion, lentils, lemon juice, salt, and thyme. Cover and simmer 1 hour or until meat and vegetables are tender, stirring occasionally. 12 cups.

THE INSTANTLY RECOGNIZABLE SOUND OF A HARLEY is as distinctive as the unmistakable flavor of a Chicago pizza. For some of the best, stop at Uno or Due. When you can't get to Chicago, make this triple-cheese likeness and imagine you're cruising the road!

Triple Cheese Pizza

1 ready-made baked pizza crust (16 ounces)
6 tablespoons pesto sauce
1 cup grated Fontina cheese (about 4 ounces)
5-6 plum tomatoes, seeded and thinly sliced
1 tablespoon dried, crumbled oregano
½ teaspoon dried basil
½ cup freshly grated mozzarella cheese, (about 2 ounces)
⅓ cup freshly grated Parmesan cheese
Black pepper to taste

Preheat oven to 450 degrees. Place pizza crust on large baking sheet. Spread with pesto. Sprinkle evenly with Fontina cheese. Arrange tomatoes over pizza. Season with oregano, basil, and black pepper. Add

mozzarella and Parmesan cheese. Bake until crust is golden and topping is bubbly, about 10-12 minutes. 4 servings.

IRISH, ITALIAN, AND EASTERN EUROPEAN IMMIGRANTS settled around Joliet and worked the river corridor between Lake Michigan and the Mississippi River for years. Hearty food and a strong ethnic heritage is evident around here. Irish coffee is traditionally American and popular in the area. Here is one way it is served to bikers in Joliet.

Joliet

Irish Coffee

½ cup whipping cream
2 teaspoons powdered sugar
1 teaspoon vanilla
8 ounces Irish whiskey or brandy
8 teaspoons brown sugar
8 cups strong, hot coffee

Whip cream with powdered sugar and vanilla. Place 1 ounce (2 tablespoons) whiskey and 1 teaspoon brown sugar into each heatproof mug; stir. Pour hot coffee into mugs and top with whipped cream. Serve immediately. 8 cups.

The Old Log Cabin Cafe

The Old Log Cabin Cafe just north of Pontiac is a stop where biker memories are made. Behind the counter, regular customers have names painted on their own coffee mugs and find them waiting on a Peg-Board behind the counter each morning. This is the Route 66 eatery that once faced the other direction on State Highway 4. When Route 66 came along, the owners decided to move the front door. They jacked up the building, turned it around and opened the front to Route 66 traffic again.

Brad and Debbie Trainor have owned the cafe since 1986. They serve plenty of good home cooking.

THE RIVIERA RESTAURANT, JUST NORTH OF GARDNER, has always attracted free spirits. It was built in 1928, the beginning of the depression years, by James Girot who hired unemployed men to move the buildings from Gardner and South Wilmington and reconstruct them to create a tavern and restaurant. The upper floor became a restaurant, the lower floor was the tavern. The old barroom remains as it was once designed — much like a cave with stalactites hanging from the ceiling.

The menu is primarily Italian, but owners Bob and Peggy Kraft also serve great steak, chicken, and seafood. They have been at the Riviera since 1972 and welcome fellow free spirits who love to stomp out conformity. Be sure to check the Riviera restrooms!

Beef Stroganoff
RIVIERA RESTAURANT

2 cups minced onion
2 large cloves minced garlic
4 tablespoons margarine
2 pounds round steak, cut into bite-sized pieces
Salt and pepper to taste
½ cup flour
1 can (10 ¾ ounces) beef broth or consommé
⅓ cup red wine
8 ounces sliced mushrooms
1 teaspoon nutmeg
2 cups sour cream
Freshly prepared noodles

Sauté onions and garlic in margarine. Set aside. Flour steak, add salt and pepper and brown in hot skillet. Deglaze pan with consommé. Combine all ingredients except sour cream and noodles. Bake in preheated 350-degree oven until tender.

Just before serving, add sour cream. Serve over noodles. Note: This can also be cooked very slowly on a surface unit of the range. 8 servings.

HUNGRY BIKERS WILL FIND A BELLY-SATISFYING DESSERT with this luscious recipe shared by Jo Ann Burns from the Exchange Bank in Gardner. Her apple squares are yummy!

Jo Ann Burns' Sour Cream Apple Squares

2 cups flour
2 cups brown sugar
½ cup butter
1 cup chopped pecans
1½ teaspoons cinnamon
1 teaspoon soda
½ teaspoon salt
1 cup sour cream
1 teaspoon vanilla
1 egg
2 cups apples, peeled and chopped

Combine flour, sugar and butter. Blend at low speed with a mixer. Stir in the nuts. Press all but 1 cup of the crumb mixture into an ungreased 9x13 pan. To remaining mixture add cinnamon, soda, salt, sour cream, vanilla and egg. Blend well. Stir in the apples. Spoon over pressed mixture. Bake in a preheated 350-degree oven for 25-30 minutes. Serve warm with ice cream or whipped cream. 10-12 servings.

Dwight

GENUINE COMFORT FOOD ALWAYS OUTLASTS THE TRENDS and has widespread appeal. This is certainly true in Dwight where ham loaves have remained popular through the years at the annual bazaar held by the United Methodist Women.

Ham Loaves

Dwight United Methodist Women

1½ pounds ground smoked ham
½ pound ground fresh pork
2 eggs, beaten
1 cup milk
1 cup cracker crumbs
½ teaspoon pepper
Extra crumbs for rolling
Sauce:
1 cup brown sugar
1 scant tablespoon dry mustard
½ cup vinegar
½ cup water

Combine ham, pork, eggs, milk, crumbs, and pepper into 8 loaves. Roll ham loaves in extra cracker crumbs and bake in a preheated oven for 15 minutes at 350 degrees. Meanwhile, combine sauce ingredients in a small saucepan and bring to a boil. Reduce oven heat to 325 degrees. Baste loaves with sauce and continue cooking for 45 minutes, basting every 5 minutes with the sauce. 8 servings.

EFFIE MARX OF DWIGHT is a member of the Illinois Route 66 Hall of Fame. She holds the distinction of being the longest working waitress on Route 66. Effie began working at an eatery in Odell in 1931 and served several generations of customers in Odell, Braidwood, Hinsdale, and finally Dwight. She signed on at Phil's Harvest Table at age sixty-two and worked there over fifteen years. Effie shared her favorite brownie recipe a short time before her death.

Effie Marx's Brownies

½ cup (1 stick) margarine at room temperature
1 cup sugar
4 eggs
1 cup flour
¼ teaspoon salt
1 can (16-ounce) Hershey's syrup
½ cup chopped nuts (optional)

Combine margarine, sugar and eggs. Beat together until well blended then add flour and salt. Stir in syrup and nuts. Bake in an 8½x11 pan in a 350 degree oven for 30 minutes.

Frosting:
½ cup margarine
1½ cups sugar
⅓ cup milk
½ cup chocolate chips

Combine margarine, sugar, and milk, and bring to boil for 30 seconds only. Remove from heat and add ½ cup chocolate chips. Beat mixture until glossy and spread on brownies.

Bill Shea's Gas Station Museum, Springfield

GLAIDA FUNK CAME TO FUNK'S GROVE by way of Oklahoma. She and her husband Steve met while he was taking pilot training in Enid during World War II. Steve's great-grandfather, Isaac, settled in the only maple grove along Route 66 just over a hundred years before the Mother Road came into being.

Glaida remembers the years after World War II as pretty primitive. She and Steve sold sirup from the back porch and met their share of hitchhikers, vagrants, and folks whose cars refused to make another mile. Often, these folks were hired on for food.

Life slowed again at Funk's Grove when the interstate opened in 1976, but eventually people found them again, and today Funk's Grove is one of the most popular stops along the highway. A jug of Funk's Grove Pure Maple Sirup in the tank bag is the mark of a seasoned roadie. Just be sure to keep the lid on tight.

Funk's Grove Maple Sirup Bars

½ cup butter
¼ cup sugar
1 cup flour
¾ cup brown sugar
⅓ cup maple sirup
1 tablespoon butter
1 egg
½ teaspoon vanilla
⅓ cup chopped pecans

Cream butter and sugar in food processor. Add flour and process until just blended. Dough does not form ball. Pat into bottom of greased 9-inch square pan. Bake at 350 degrees for 15 minutes, or until lightly browned. Beat brown sugar, syrup, and butter to blend. Beat in egg and vanilla. Pour over shortbread. Sprinkle with nuts. Bake 25 minutes or until set. Cool and cut into bars. 2 dozen bars.

Bikers pause for visit with Debby Funk (front, left) at Funk's Grove

15

GLAIDA FUNK SAYS THAT ALMA VAN NESS was one of the best cooks in McLean. She and her husband, Archie, lived on the corner of Route 66 and Highway 136 from 1938 until 1969. The corner was known as the "death corner" because of many accidents occurred there. The location today is home to a McDonald's Restaurant and is across from the Dixie Truckers' Home. Could any biker resist a warm slab of rhubarb pie topped with a big dollop of authentic whipped cream?

Dixie Truckers Home, McLean

Rhubarb Pie

Crust:

3 cups flour
1 cup shortening
1 teaspoon salt
9-10 tablespoons cold water

Mix flour, shortening, and salt until consistency of corn meal. Add water as needed. Roll and shape into 9-inch pie pans. Enough for 2 double-crust pies or 4 single-crust pies.

Filling:

3 cups rhubarb
3 tablespoons flour
1½ cups sugar
Dash of cinnamon
2 eggs, well-beaten
1 tablespoon melted butter

Place rhubarb in unbaked 9-inch crust. Combine flour, sugar, cinnamon, eggs and butter. Mix well. Pour over rhubarb. Put on top crust, seal and cut air vents. Bake in a preheated 350 degree oven for 1 hour. Yields 6-8 slices.

IN THE SUMMER OF 1996, employees of the Lehn and Fink Company in Lincoln published a cookbook sharing treasured recipes from those who worked for the company from the time it opened in 1947 until the doors closed forever. Bert Marten shared this comfortable main dish, as gratifying as the growl of a favorite Harley engine.

Stuffed Manicotti

Lasting Memories Cookbook

1½ pounds lean hamburger
½ cup chopped onion
½ teaspoon garlic salt
1 teaspoon salt
Pepper to taste

1 cup dry bread crumbs
1 tablespoon dried parsley flakes
½ pound grated mozzarella cheese
2 eggs
½ cup milk
14 manicotti shells
1 jar (28-ounce) pasta sauce

Brown hamburger with onion, salt and pepper. Drain and allow to cool slightly. Pour into mixing bowl and add bread crumbs, parsley, cheese, eggs, and milk. Mix thoroughly. Cook the manicotti according to package directions. Stuff each shell with the meat mixture. Place in a 9x11 baking dish and cover with pasta sauce. Bake in 350-degree oven for 30 minutes. This manicotti freezes well. 14 shells.

THESE GINGERSNAPS ARE GUARANTEED to provide the gumption for a great ride.

Gingersnaps
Lasting Memories Cookbook

1 cup white sugar
¾ cup margarine or shortening
1 egg
4 tablespoons dark molasses
2 cups flour
2 teaspoons soda
1 teaspoon ginger
1 teaspoon cinnamon
1 teaspoon cloves

Mix sugar and shortening. Add egg and mix. Add molasses and mix well. Add flour, soda, and spices. Make balls the size of walnuts; roll in granulated sugar. Spray cookie sheet with nonstick cooking spray. Bake in preheated 350-degree oven for 15 minutes. 3 dozen cookies.

ERNIE AND FRAN EDWARDS LOVE TO VISIT. The famous Pig Hip Restaurant is closed now, but Ernie and Illinois Route 66 faithfuls have turned the old place into a great highway museum. Take time to visit, exchange autographs, pick up some souvenirs, sign the guest book, and hear a few road stories firsthand.

Pig-Hip Restaurant, Broadwell

When I stopped to see if Ernie and Fran would share a recipe or memory for the book, they promised to give it some thought and put a note in the mail. A few days after I returned home, Ernie's letter came. He shared two memories:

17

"This sandwich was not a successful one but it was good. I made the Chick Burger back in 1942. I used a five-pound chicken and boiled it 'till the meat fell off the bone then shredded it real well. Then I made a real creamy coleslaw. Put the meat on a bun, add coleslaw, and that five-pound chicken would serve fifty sandwiches."

Ernie says another sandwich that was popular was his "Yip-Yap." It was a hot dog bun that had one end cut off. Ernie made a hole in the end, filled the bun with chili meat and served it like an ice cream cone. He said it was good and "rather successful."

Fran and Ernie Edwards, owners of Pig-Hip Restaurant

ENJOY SMALL-TOWN PEACE AND QUIET IN WILLIAMSVILLE, where Edie Senalik specializes in homemade bagels and Italian biscotti. Pack some along to chow down with a cup of authentic highway coffee — as black as the midnight sky.

Edie's Biscotti Di Pratto

¼ cup blanched almonds
¾ cup natural whole almonds
3 eggs
1 teaspoon vanilla
¼ teaspoon almond extract
2¼ cups all-purpose flour
1 cup sugar
1 teaspoon baking soda
Pinch of salt
1 egg

Preheat oven to 350 degrees. On a baking sheet, roast both kinds of almonds until blanched almonds start to brown, shaking occasionally, 5-8 minutes. Remove blanched almonds, place in blender or food processor to pulverize. Set aside.

Return whole almonds to oven for 2-3 minutes longer. Remove and chop roughly. Set aside.

Reduce heat in oven to 300 degrees. Grease and dust a baking sheet. Set aside. In a small bowl, beat the eggs, vanilla, and almond extract together. In a larger bowl, mix flour, sugar, baking soda, salt, and pulverized almonds. Make a well in center and add egg mixture, blending until stiff dough is formed. Add a few drops of water if mixture does not hold together. Add chopped almonds and knead to evenly distribute.

Divide dough into 3 portions. Form each into a long round, slightly oval log, about 1½ inches in diameter.

Place on baking sheet. Beat remaining egg and brush onto log surfaces.

Bake at 300 degrees for 45 minutes.

Remove from oven and allow to rest for 5 minutes. Turn oven to 275 degrees. With serrated knife, cut logs into ¼-inch slices. Lay biscotti flat on two cookie sheets. Return to oven for 20 minutes, turning over half-way through baking time. Allow to cool before sealing in containers. Will stay fresh for up to a month. These crusty morsels are good to dip in coffee. 6-7 dozen.

SUE WALDMIRE OWNS AND OPERATES the Cozy Dog Drive-In and Supply Company in Springfield.

Ed Waldmire, the originator of the Cozy Dog, opened this Springfield icon in 1949. Virginia, Ed's wife, designed the famous logo of the two hot dogs embracing. Bob Waldmire, the road's favorite cruising artist, is Sue's brother-in-law.

Chili

COZY DOG DRIVE-IN AND SUPPLY COMPANY

1 pound red beans
2 quarts water
2 tablespoons Cozy Dog Drive-In Chili Mix
2 cups beef suet, melted and strained
1 onion
1 green pepper
1 pound lean ground beef
½ cup chili spice
1 small can tomato paste

Cook the beans in the water with the chili mix until they are tender. Meanwhile, heat the suet and dice the onion and pepper. Sauté until soft. Add ground beef and continue cooking and stirring until meat is browned and crumbly. Add chili spice and tomato paste. Bring to boil.

To serve, add beans to each bowl then cover with meat sauce.

Note: The secret to the success of this recipe is to serve warmed, and crisp oyster crackers with each steaming bowl.

FOR THOSE WHO PREFER A VEGETARIAN CHILI, here is an adaptation that would please Bob Waldmire. You don't have to be a vegetarian to enjoy this filling meal!

Vegetarian Black Bean Chili

4 cups dried, rinsed, black beans
Water to cover
2 tablespoons olive oil
1 large onion, chopped
2 green bell peppers, chopped
6 large garlic cloves, minced
2 tablespoons cumin
2 tablespoons chili powder
2 teaspoons dried basil
1 teaspoon dried oregano
½ teaspoon cayenne pepper
2 4-ounce cans diced green chilies, undrained
½ cup tomato sauce
¼ cup fresh lime juice

Toppings:
Chopped tomatoes and onions
Grated cheese
Sour cream
Avocado slices
Crackers

Place beans in large pot. Add cold water to cover at least 3 inches. Soak overnight. Drain beans, reserving 3 cups of the liquid. Return beans to pot and add cold water again to cover. Simmer beans until tender, about 2 to 2½ hours. Drain.

Heat oil in heavy pan. Add onions, bell pepper, garlic, cumin, chili, basil, oregano, and cayenne and cook approximately 10 minutes. Add beans, reserved soaking liquid, chilies, and tomato sauce. Stir and cook slowly until chili is thick, about 45 minutes. Add lime juice and season with salt and pepper to taste. Serve in bowls and pass toppings. 12 servings.

Veteran biker Jamie Constantine enjoys an ear of sweet corn

THE VILLAGE OF DIVERNON is a small agricultural community that experienced a spurt of growth at the turn of the century due to mining, then quickly returned to a quiet, comfortable township. Their *Centennial Cookbook, 1900-2000* is a treasure of regional food. Here is a fine example, offering deep-down satisfaction and pure comfort. What more could a biker want?

Bev Kalaskie's Italian Beef

4 to 5 pounds beef roast (Use chuck or arm roast.)
1 teaspoon oregano
2 beef bouillon cubes
1 teaspoon fennel
½ teaspoon nutmeg
1 large onion, sliced

1 clove garlic or 1 teaspoon garlic powder
Pinch of basil
¼ teaspoon allspice
½ teaspoon pepper
2 bay leaves
¼ teaspoon thyme
½ teaspoon dried parsley
1 teaspoon salt
2 cups water

Preheat oven to 325 degrees. Place meat in a roaster, combine then add all ingredients. Cover with lid and roast meat for 20 minutes per pound. When the meat has cooled, slice it and return to roaster with remaining juices. Add extra water if necessary. Warm again and serve with kaiser rolls. Note: All spices can be adjusted to personal taste.

4 servings per pound of meat.

GRACE AND ROGER BROWN, ALONG WITH THEIR DAUGHTER and son-in-law, Debra and Darry Lucas, bought Art's Cafe in Farmersville in 1978. This Route 66 classic stop has a long history of satisfying 66 bikers. That going-away growl of satisfied Harley owners is just a little more comforting after a satisfying piece of this butterscotch pie.

Debbie's Butterscotch Pie

1 cup brown sugar
1½ cups water
1½ cups milk, scalded
4 tablespoons cornstarch
4 tablespoons flour
½ teaspoon salt

3 egg yolks, beaten
4 tablespoons butter
1 teaspoon vanilla
1 10-inch baked pie shell

Meringue:
3 egg whites
2 tablespoon sugar

Mix brown sugar with water in a medium saucepan and bring to a boil. Add scalded milk. Combine cornstarch, flour, and salt. Carefully stir into sugar, water, and milk mixture and cook until thick, stirring constantly. Add egg yolks and butter and cook an additional 2 minutes. Stir in vanilla. Pour pie into a baked 10-inch crust. Whip egg whites and add sugar, beating until glossy.

Cover pie with meringue. Bake in a preheated 350-degree oven until meringue is lightly browned, about 12-15 minutes. 7-8 slices.

ONE OF THE BEST OF THE ROUTE 66 FEED STOPS is Litchfield's Ariston Cafe. In its present location since 1935, the cafe is operated by Nick and Demi Adam. Nick is the son of the founder, Pete Adam, who originally opened the restaurant in nearby Carlinville in 1925. The restaurant is known for quality food and a warm welcome. Nick and Demi are proud of their Greek heritage and shared this time-honored dessert favorite. The Ariston Cafe is a favorite biker stop, recommended by all who have enjoyed the friendly service.

Ariston Cafe, Litchfield

Baklava
ARISTON CAFE

Syrup:
2 cups water
3 cups sugar
1 teaspoon lemon
2 cinnamon sticks

In a medium saucepan, combine all ingredients. Bring to a boil; simmer 15 minutes or until candy thermometer registers 224 degrees. Remove from heat; cool; remove cinnamon sticks.

Nut filling:
1½ cups sugar
2 pounds walnuts, chopped
2 teaspoons cinnamon
Dash of ground clove

In a medium bowl, stir together nuts, sugar, cinnamon, and cloves. Set aside.

Phyllo preparation:
1 package of phyllo dough
3 sticks of butter

Open phyllo and place sheets between pieces of wax paper. Cover loosely with damp towel so phyllo won't dry out. In a small saucepan, melt butter and keep warm. Brush bottom of a 9x13 or 13-inch round pan (not glass) with melted butter. Line pan with 3 sheets of phyllo, brushing each sheet with melted butter. Sprinkle with a handful of nut mixture. Place another sheet of phyllo on top of nuts, brushing each sheet with butter. Repeat this procedure until all nut mixture is used.

Top with 3 or 4 remaining phyllo sheets, brushing each with melted butter while layering one on top of the other.

With the tip of a sharp knife, carefully cut or score all layers of baklava into desired size. Do not cut or score all the way through the phyllo.

Bake at 350 degrees for 45-50 minutes or until golden brown. Remove from oven and while still hot, carefully spoon cooled syrup evenly over the baklava. 12-15 servings.

THE VOLUNTEER AUXILIARY at Litchfield's St. Francis Hospital produced *A Taste of St. Francis* several years ago. After enjoying these two great dishes from their collection, you may need a nap before taking to the road again!

Honey Sesame Tenderloin
A Taste of St. Francis

1 pound pork tenderloin
½ cup soy sauce

2 cloves minced garlic
1 tablespoon grated ginger
1 tablespoon sesame oil
¼ cup honey
2 tablespoons brown sugar
4 tablespoons sesame seed

Place tenderloin in a plastic bag. Combine soy sauce, garlic, ginger, and sesame oil; pour soy mixture over meat. Marinate overnight in refrigerator. Remove pork from marinade. Mix honey and brown sugar in shallow plate. Roll pork in mixture, coating all sides. Place in roasting pan and sprinkle with sesame seeds. Roast at 375 degrees for 20-30 minutes or until meat thermometer reaches 160 degrees. 4 servings.

Potato Puffs
A Taste of St. Francis

3 cups hot mashed potatoes
4 tablespoons butter or margarine, melted
1 cup bread crumbs
⅓ cup low-fat mayonnaise
1 teaspoon salt
½ teaspoon dried basil
1 tablespoon grated lemon peel
1½ teaspoons lemon juice
1 cup milk
3 eggs, separated
¼ cup grated cheddar cheese

Litchfield Cafe

CAUTION: We Brake for ROUTE 66 Historic Sites

Combine melted margarine with crumbs; spread in shallow 9-inch casserole. Combine mayonnaise, salt, basil, lemon peel and juice, milk, and beaten egg yolk. Add to mashed potatoes; beat until smooth and fluffy. Beat egg whites until stiff; fold into potato mixture. Pour into casserole. Sprinkle with cheese. Bake in preheated 300 degree oven for 30 minutes. Turn oven to 375 degrees and bake 10 minutes longer or until browned. 6 servings.

THE ITALIAN INFLUENCE CAN STILL BE FELT in many of the dishes prepared in the southern Illinois community of Edwardsville. Folks around here enjoy their food, fun, and freedom almost as much as bikers. Barb Driesner, a member of the staff at the Edwardsville Library, says her mostaccioli recipe is typical of the area.

Barb Driesner's Mostaccioli

1 pound hamburger
1 pound Italian sausage
1 onion, diced
1 box (12 ounces) rigatoni or mostaccioli noodles
1 jar (28-ounce) Italian pasta sauce
8 ounces mozzarella cheese, grated
1 teaspoon garlic powder

Brown the hamburger and sausage with the onion. Drain thoroughly. Add sauce and garlic powder. Meanwhile, cook the rigatoni noodles. Layer ½ of the meat mixture in the bottom of a 9x13 inch baking dish. Cover with the noodles and half of the cheese. Repeat with remaining meat. Sprinkle remaining cheese on top. Bake uncovered in a preheated 350-degree oven for 30 minutes until mixture is hot and bubbly. 8 servings.

COLLINSVILLE IS THE HORSERADISH CAPITAL OF THE WORLD. Over 60 percent of the world's supply of the spicy herb is grown in the bottomlands around Collinsville. So naturally, many of the favorite dishes prepared by the good cooks around here include horseradish. This tasty recipe for chicken wings was shared for the McLean, Texas, recipe book, *Cuisine Down Old Route 66*.

Mississzippy Wings

Cuisine Down Old Route 66

4 pounds chicken wings
½ cup prepared horseradish
½ cup catsup
¼ cup sugar
⅓ cup lemon-lime soda
¼ cup water
2 tablespoons cooking oil
½ teaspoon garlic salt
¼ teaspoon pepper

Wash, then remove and discard tip sections of 4 pounds of chicken wings. Put wings in a small bowl. Combine remaining ingredients and pour mixture over wings, making sure all are covered. Cover bowl and refrigerate overnight. Remove wings and place on foil-lined shallow baking pan. Bake in preheated 350 degree oven for 1 hour or until wings are well done and crispy.

Turning and basting after the first ½ hour assures more even crispness. Dispose of excess marinade. About 24 wings.

SAY GOODBYE TO ILLINOIS at the historic Chain of Rocks Bridge.

Boys of Summer

— MICHAEL WALLIS

Beyond the Chicago sprawl, out in the Illinois countryside with its tidy farms and fields and grain elevators, bikers feel like they're riding through a giant version of a model train landscape. Out here, with acres of licorice-colored earth all around and the promise of more adventure around the next curve and bend, it becomes clear why Route 66 attracts so many bikers. If ever a path was made to order for a Harley it's this one.

Original Route 66 in Illinois

I figured that out some years ago, when I made the whole east-to-west journey on the old road and devoted almost a month to cruising from Chicago to Santa Monica. On this Route 66 journey I rode with a big posse of Harley riders including a bunch from several European countries. They had shipped their bikes to Chicago and I was invited to tag along. I didn't need to be asked twice.

Bikers gather at the Launching Pad, Wilmington

By late morning, after we passed through Berwyn, Willowbrook, and Romeoville, we stopped for cold drinks in Wilmington at the Launching Pad Drive-In, where a towering fiberglass spaceman giant stands guard in the parking lot. Just a short while later, we were all ready to stop again. This time it was the little highway burg of Odell. We wanted to pay our respects at the beautifully restored 1930s gas station that has become one of the true icons of the Mother Road.

Restored Standard Oil gasoline station, Odell

Fueled by a stout breakfast at Lou Mitchell's, the famed eatery located near the start of Route 66 in the Chicago Loop, we cruised out of the city as fast as we could. It was a hodgepodge of riders — men, women, young and old. There were retired execs, judges, doctors, priests, a stand-up comic, blue bloods, red necks, poets, and probably a few ex-cons. It really didn't matter. We never talked about our work anyway. The ride was what counted. That was really all that any of us cared about.

We slowed to a crawl after coming to the sign marking the town limits and cruised beneath the canopy of trees lining the shoulders of the highway until we reached the gas station perched on a gentle curve. After parking in the shade of a tree we crossed the highway to take a closer look at the vintage filling station that had been brought back to it's original state by the diligent road warriors of Illinois. Some citizens turned out to greet us including the town mayor and a few of the grassroots preservationists who had put so much time and sweat equity into the restoration of the building.

The tour only took a few minutes leaving us plenty of time to gulp down big glasses of freshly made lemonade provided by the locals. I finished my drink and was making my way back to the bikes along with a chap from France who was taking his dream trip down Route 66 in order to discover the America he had heard about all his life. We crossed the highway just as a pair of little boys — about ten years old — appeared on their bicycles. They proceeded to show off their riding skills, doing wheelies and other tricks, and then they rode around us in circles that grew tighter and tighter until they stopped next to us. Baseball cards were secured by clothespins to the bicycle spokes and ball gloves adorned the handlebars.

These were true boys of summer, complete with grass stained blue jean, tee shirts, rings of dirt around their necks, and hot weather burr haircuts. They also were obviously curious about us but too shy to speak. I broke the ice and asked them if they were from Odell.

Bikers meet locals at Odell

"Yes, sir," they shot back in unison.

That was all they needed. A flood of questions poured forth from the boys. They wanted to know where we came from and where we were going and all the while they talked they looked us up and down and shot envious looks at our motorcycles parked nearby.

They were in utter awe and also disbelief that so many bikers would come to their little town of Odell and actually stop to look at some old building. Neither of the boys had ever been to St. Louis or Chicago.

"This is the most exciting day of our lives!" one of the boys blurted out to us. "We've never seen so many motorcycles and people."

"We've been here all our lives," the other boy offered. "This is the most boring town in the world."

Then they asked us for our autographs and each one pulled a baseball card from the spokes and thrust them toward us. My riding companion produced a pen and we scribbled our signatures. But before the boys could ride away with their treasure I stopped them with a question.

"So boys, you think your town here is boring?"

They nodded .

"Don't you two guys know where you live?"

"Well Odell," they shot back in unison as if I was nuts.

"I know that but there's something more you boys need to realize," I told them. "You live on the most famous highway in the whole world. You live on Route 66. There's no other highway like this one and there is no other town quite like Odell. You have something special here and that makes you special."

The boys' eyes got big as pie plates.

"You boys live on a road that will take you not only to St. Louis and Chicago but way beyond. It's right here just waiting for you. And the good part is that in the meantime the world — and I mean the whole world — will come to you. That's why I came and so did this man here — he's come all the way from Paris, France, just to see your town and to meet you boys."

The boys looked at each other but did not speak.

"Be good to this old town and this road," I continued. "This road is a true legend and always remember that it can take you anyplace you want to go."

Then I asked them to give us *their* autographs. They were stunned but reached down and removed two more baseball cards from the spokes. They carefully signed their names and handed them to the French biker and me. We bid them *adieu* and fired up our Harleys.

We were a long way down the highway — almost out of sight — when I glanced in my mirror and saw the boys standing in the same spot. They were still waving. I knew they'd never forget our meeting. Neither would I. ∎

The Legend

— MICHAEL WALLIS

Route 66 has always meant going somewhere. Just ask any biker who has made the journey and you will quickly understand.

Since 1926, this ribbon of asphalt and concrete has connected travelers — including legions of bikers — to the fabric of the land. It has carried us from the heart of America, through the romantic West of our imagination to the golden shores of California. We could follow our dreams of adventure, or seek a better life.

No other highway has been so immortalized in song, prose, or film. Route 66 offered early travelers the sights and sounds of America at its best. Today it invites us to revisit the country as it was before it became generic. The road transports us back to a time when the landscape was not littered with cookie-cutter houses, franchise eateries, and shopping malls peddling look-alike merchandise to people in danger of losing their own identity.

Route 66 is an event in itself. Road lore, handed down through the generations, is still being shared, and passed along by travelers adding to the legend as they urge others to follow.

The Route 66 I love puts me in touch with my roots and myself. It is a highway of phantoms and dreams reaching beyond a destination on the map.

Enjoy the odyssey! ∎

Missouri

Fast Facts from Missouri

- Route 66 mileage in Missouri — 317

- Missouri wines are among the best in the nation.

- Missouri roads are made for bikers, take some side trips to feel the pulse of this vibrant state.

- Hooker Cut, east of Devil's Elbow, is one of the deepest rock cuts in the country.

- Missouri is one of only two states which borders eight other states.

- One of the first concrete paved portions of the Missouri highway system connected Carthage to Joplin in 1920. This road became part of Route 66 in 1926.

St. Louis Gateway Arch casts its shadow on the park below

Missouri Biker Road Rules

- Safety Helmet, required by law

- Eye Protection, not required

Must see in Missouri

- ST. LOUIS, "GATEWAY TO THE WEST"
  - 630-foot-high Gateway Arch, downtown riverfront
  - Anheuser-Busch Brewery, I-55 at Arsenal St.
  - Museum of Transportation, 3015 Barrett Station Road

- STANTON — Meramec Caverns

- ST. JAMES
  - Rosati Winery, the oldest active winery along 66, 22050 State Route KK
  - St. James Winery, 540 Sydney Street

- ROLLA — Memoryville USA, a lavish classic car museum and antique stop

- SPRINGFIELD
  - Bass Pro Shop
  - Begin in Springfield to drive a long segment of original Route 66 without interstate interruptions — all the way to Oklahoma City. The drive includes that original nine foot-wide Route 66 ribbon in two segments between Miami and Afton in Oklahoma.

Where to buy stuff

- Route 66 Motors and General Store, 12661 Old Hwy. 66, east of Rolla

- Wrink's Food Market, City Route 66 East, Lebanon (across from the Munger Moss Motel)

The Show Me State

Beacons in the dark

- CUBA — Wagon Wheel Motel, 901 East Washington

- ROLLA — Zeno's Motel, Route 66, 1621 Martin Spring Dr.

- LEBANON — Munger Moss Motel, Route 66, 236 Seminole

- SPRINGFIELD — Best Western Rail Haven, 203 S. Glenstone Ave.

Favorite hangouts for food and drink

- ST. LOUIS
  - TED DREWES FROZEN CUSTARD, 6726 Chippewa
  - BLUEBERRY HILLS CAFE, 6504 Delmar Ave. (not on 66 but worth a trip). Among many other awards, voted the "Best Hamburgers," "Best Restroom Graffiti," and "Best Jukebox in America."
  - JAKE'S STEAKS, at Laclede's Landing, 707 Clamorgan

- KIRKWOOD — MASSA'S, 210 N. Kirkwood

- PACIFIC
  - RED CEDAR INN, 1047 East Osage
  - ROUTE 66 DINER, 409 East Osage

- VILLA RIDGE — TRI-COUNTY TRUCK STOP, I-44 & Highway 100, Exit 251

- SULLIVAN — HOMER'S HICKORY-SMOKED BBQ, 693 Fisher (Locals say this is the best barbecue in the area.)

Wagon Wheel Motel, Cuba

33

- *CUBA*
  - THE FEED LOT, east of Cuba at Exit 209 from I-44
  - MISSOURI HICKORY BAR-B-Q, 913 East Washington

- *ST. JAMES* — DOUGLAS COMPANY, 601 Hwy. B

- *ROLLA*
  - BRUNO'S, 2001 Forum Drive
  - JOHNNY'S SMOKE STAK, 201 Highway 72W (Good barbecue!)
  - A SLICE OF PIE, Route 66 and US 63

- *DEVIL'S ELBOW* — ELBOW INN BAR AND BBQ PIT (another great biker stop), at the bridge on the 1926 alignment

- *LEBANON* — STONEGATE STATION, 1475 S. Jefferson

- *MARSHFIELD* — TINY'S SMOKEHOUSE, 77 State Hwy W.

- *SPRINGFIELD*
  - LAMBERT'S CAFE "Home of the Throwed Rolls", 7 miles south on Hwy. 65

  - HEMINGWAY'S BLUE WATER CAFE, US 60 and Sunshine Street in Bass Pro Shop
  - STEAK 'N SHAKE, 4 locations
  - LAST GREAT AMERICAN DINER, 507 Carney

- *CARTHAGE*
  - CARTHAGE DELI AND ICE CREAM, 301 S. Main (northwest corner of town square)
  - C.D.'S PANCAKE HUT, 301 S. Garrison

- *WEBB CITY* — BRADBURY BISHOP DELI AND ROUTE 66 DINER, in an 1887 building at 201 N. Main

- *JOPLIN*
  - BENITO'S MEXICAN RESTAURANT, for good Mexican food, 2525 Range Line Road
  - FRED AND RED'S, South Main

Devils' Elbow

Riding for Rainbows

— MICHAEL WALLIS

It had rained hard for two days all the way down Route 66 through Illinois and across the Mississippi River into Missouri but we figured the worst was done. The eye of the storm missed us. Now only a lingering but light rain fell — not enough to postpone our trip or force us beneath an overpass for cover. We checked out of the hotel, pulled on rain gear, and fired up the bikes. Then we jumped right into the morning traffic of St. Louis.

The night before, despite the rain, we had ridden out to Ted Drewes Frozen Custard, a legendary Mother Road stop in St. Louis. It was well worth the wet ride. No demons emerged on the slick streets and Ted himself was there to greet us and share some road stories while we devoured cups of frosty ambrosia. Now with a good night's sleep and a few mugs of coffee we were anxious to get back on the old road as soon as possible. If only the sun would appear.

Our band of bikers knew the rain drill. There is nothing like wet feet and cold water pouring into your crotch to take away your edge and make you miserable. Everyone in our bunch, however, had good rainsuits,

Ted Drewes Frozen Custard, St. Louis

understood the principle of traction, and made damn sure every car and truck around saw us. Also we all had a sense of humor. That always goes a long way.

The bikes' headlights reflected on a river of rain beneath the wheels and we literally flowed out of St. Louis. At least the slippery oil and road gunk had been washed off the pavement after so much rain. Ever optimistic, we searched for sunshine but our first mission was to clear the city and then find hot food and comfort.

We stuck to the super slab — Interstate 44 — to jump start the day and reach more riding room out on the old road. We zipped along at a steady clip until we came to the Six Flags exit. We glided down the off-ramp, turned under the super slab on Allenton Road, and then hooked the first right. We were back on Route 66. Several of my pals raised their fists in triumphant salutes.

The rain still came down but everyone felt better. Now we were on the Mother Road. We could set our pace, call the shots, and ride like we were meant to ride.

Just ahead waited the old highway and railroad town of Pacific. I had known Pacific since I was a kid and my folks took Sunday

35

drives this way. It was where I bought my first car — a shiny black '55 Plymouth Savoy clean as a newborn — from an elderly lady, its original owner.

I recalled the times when I had stopped along the high bluffs bordering the highway and climbed the steep trail leading to a scenic overview named Jensen Point. Although that vantagepoint overlooking Route 66 and the surrounding countryside was now fenced off I knew that my initials and those of some of my pals were carved in the wooden beams of the stone pavilion at the summit.

Now on this rainy morning, riding on with stomachs growling, my Harley group would have eagerly stopped for a hot meal at the Red Cedar Inn, one of the best-known restaurants on the entire route, if it had been open. But the Red Cedar, built from logs and love in 1934, only offers lunch and dinner. Had we been there later in the day, or at twilight, we would have pulled in for plates filled with catfish, liver and onions, real mashed spuds, chicken and dumplings, and bread pudding so tasty diners often lick the bowls clean.

Once in town, we slowed and scanned for a breakfast stop amidst the residences and commerce flanking both sides of the road. Then we saw a cluster of bikes and pickups parked at a World War II-style Quonset hut. We followed suit and splashed through the puddles to join them.

It was a cafe named DJ's, for Delissa and Joye. Inside it was warm as toast and there were just enough empty places to accommodate our crew. We greeted our fellow bikers as well as some local people and a trucker whose rig was parked outside. We were all together as one, out of the rain and sharing a few moments together.

DJ's was warm and cozy and the waitresses lost no time handing out dishtowels so we could wipe off the rain. Next came the coffee and food orders. The jukebox sported some decent tunes and was set at just the right sound level. The aroma of sizzling bacon perfumed the place and within no time we were tangling with platters of hot cakes and fried eggs.

When I went to the men's toilet and passed the kitchen, a fry cook smiled and said, "Remember, you can't have rainbows without both sun and rain." She gave me a wink and went back to work at the griddle.

It was a meal I have always treasured but then those seemingly simple times often produce our best memories. A band of brothers and sisters enjoying each other's company inside a snug corrugated metal hut on the side of the road. For an hour, we had died and gone to heaven.

Shelter from rain at DJ's Cafe, Pacific

We paid at the cash register and said our farewells to folks we would never again see. Outside the rain still came down but somehow that did not matter. We headed westward in search of the sun and maybe a rainbow. ∎

Biker Weddings

— MICHAEL WALLIS

It has been said that if you encounter Michael Wallis out on Route 66, that I can marry you and your chosen. According to road lore I am like a ship's captain and may perform such nuptials. My sole caveat is that the marriage is only valid for 48 hours — a pleasant weekender.

To date, only one couple has taken me up on this standing offer. They were bikers — a couple from Boston riding Route 66. I performed the ceremony on a hotel patio in Albuquerque with scores of fellow bikers as witnesses. The happy pair rode off in the sunset on their decorated motorcycle. All of us cheered and had a grand ol' time. That was some years back. The couple no longer rides together, but their Route 66 nuptials were a highlight moment on the Mother Road that year.

Bikers who want to get legally hitched on the Main Street of America simply need to check on local wedding rules and regs, hunt up a preacher or justice of the peace, or go to the Internet for a biker-wedding specialist. There are plenty of options for locations. Really anyplace that appeals to the couple will work just fine. Here are some places to consider for your Mother Road biker wedding as suggested by both bikers and Route 66 aficionados. Unless otherwise noted, receptions may be staged at the wedding site.

- *ILLINOIS*
  - Grant Park, Chicago, with reception at Lou Mitchells
  - Our Lady of the Highways statue, west of Raymond, with reception at the Ariston Cafe, Litchfield
  - Church at Funk's Grove
  - The Cozy Dog, Springfield

- *Missouri*
  - Bridge at Devil's Elbow, with reception at Elbow Inn and honeymoon at Munger Moss Motel, Lebanon
  - Chain of Rocks Bridge, St. Louis, with on-site reception catered by Ted Drewes Frozen Custard
  - Meramec Caverns, Stanton

- *KANSAS*
  - Rainbow Bridge, near Baxter Springs, with reception at Cafe on the Route, Baxter Springs

- *OKLAHOMA*
  - Round Barn, Arcadia, with reception at nearby Hillbillies Cafe
  - Hillbillies Cafe Chapel, with reception at nearby Round Barn
  - The Sandhills Curiosity Shop, Erick, with music provided by Harley and Annabelle, "The Mediocre Music Makers"

- *TEXAS*
  - Cadillac Ranch, west of Amarillo, with reception at the Big Texan Steak Ranch, Amarillo
  - Mid-point Cafe, Adrian, ceremony outside at sign and reception in the cafe
  - Giant Cross, Groom

- *NEW MEXICO*
  - Summit of La Bajada, west of Santa Fe (warning: difficult to reach on a bike; maybe the base of the hill is better)
  - On the old road at Glenrio, with honeymoon at the Blue Swallow Motel, Tucumcari
  - Old Town Plaza, Albuquerque

- *ARIZONA*
  - Along the winding road leading to Oatman
  - Beale Hotel (site of the Clark Gable-Carol Lombard wedding), Kingman, with reception at the Oatman Hotel
  - On the Corner in Winslow, with reception and honeymoon at La Posada, Winslow

- *CALIFORNIA*
  - Iron Hog Saloon, a biker favorite, Oro Grande
  - Old townsite of Bagdad, with reception at the Bagdad Cafe, Newberry Springs
  - Santa Monica Pier, Santa Monica

Biker Road Wisdom

Gleaned from a variety of sources and old scooter tramps

Life begins on the off-ramp.

The best view of a thunderstorm is in the rearview mirror.

Bugs are tastiest at midnight.

Hot coffee and fresh pie are as important as gasoline.

When you are on a bike you are invisible.

Reheat cold burgers or burritos by strapping them to an exhaust pipe and riding 20 miles.

If you haven't ridden in rain, you've never ridden.

Keep the rubber side down and the shiny side up.

Everything is better in the wind.

Never spit when you're riding lead.

Never argue with an 18-wheeler.

There are only two kinds of bikers — those who have gone down and those who will be going down.

Good Mother Road coffee should be interchangeable with 50 weight motor oil.

Bikes parked out front of a Route 66 cafe mean good eats inside.

If you insist on riding like there's no tomorrow, there won't be.

There are drunken bikers and there are old bikers but there are no old drunken bikers.

Only open road bikers understand why dogs stick their heads out of car windows.

Do not be afraid of slowing down.

Recipes from Missouri

— MARIAN CLARK

In St. Louis, the Gateway Arch presides over the downtown waterfront. This is a dynamic city filled with opportunity: sporting events, theme parks, ethnic restaurants, river life, history, parks, and much more. The city hosted the 1904 Louisiana Purchase Centennial Exposition and World's Fair where ice cream cones and hot dogs were introduced. Iced tea and Dr. Pepper gained popularity at this great exposition as well. Busch Beer, Vess Beverages, and Ted Drewes Frozen Custard characterize St. Louis food and drink today.

At Doc's Harley-Davidson, I-44 in Kirkwood, you'll feel the Harley aura, find a warm welcome, and learn all

you want to know about biker-friendly routes through the Ozarks. Owner Pat Bush says customer relations make or break a business, so at Doc's customers are always welcomed and questions are answered.

Doc's Harley-Davidson, Kirkwood

Pat is no novice to the business. Her father started Doc's in 1955 and she has been riding since she was fifteen. Under her leadership, the business now employees forty-seven and has grown to number nine in the nation in sales. Pat is also a hands-on businesswoman. She dresses in Harley-Davidson clothes every day and rides her own Harley to work. Behind her desk is a sign: "No Cry Babies!"

Bush says women are the newest Harley market. "They're a well-balanced motorcycle, making them easier for women to ride," she said. She also offers a piece of advice to anyone interested in trying a bike, or any other new venture: "Anybody can do anything they put their mind to whether they are male or female."

When bikers gather for grub around this bustling agency, these double-stuffed potatoes are always popular.

Doc's Double-Stuffed Potatoes

4 large baking potatoes
2 tablespoons butter or margarine
½ cup chopped onion
¾ cup shredded cheeses — cheddar, provolone, or Swiss
¼ cup sour cream
2 teaspoons fresh chives
Salt and pepper to taste

Scrub potatoes; pat dry. Pierce each potato several times with a fork. Microwave on high for about 10 minutes; rotate potatoes. Microwave until tender, about 3 minutes longer.

Preheat oven to 350 degrees. Melt margarine or butter in skillet and add onion. Cook until onion is translucent, about 5 minutes.

Slice off potato tops. Scoop out potatoes, keeping shells intact; place pulp in medium bowl. Mash potatoes, add onion, ½ cup of the cheese, sour cream, chives, and salt and pepper. Blend thoroughly and spoon potato mixture back into shells, dividing evenly. Sprinkle potatoes with remaining cheese. Place on a baking sheet and put in oven for 10 minutes or until potatoes are heated through. Add bacon pieces or broccoli bits for a delicious alternative. This recipe can be enlarged easily. 4 servings.

BIKERS FEEL RIGHT AT HOME AT THE RED CEDAR INN, a sturdy building built as a cafe in 1934. Ginger Gallagher, granddaughter of the original owner, delights in serving her customers the good food they have grown to expect. There's also a friendly bar — but don't think you've imbibed too much when you see the tree that helps support the ceiling in the dining room.

Red Cedar Inn Restaurant, Pacific

Bread Pudding
RED CEDAR INN

1 box raised donuts (12 donuts)
1 cup sugar*
1 quart milk
1 teaspoon nutmeg
1 teaspoon cinnamon
6 eggs, beaten
½ cup raisins (optional)

Crumble donuts in a 2-quart baking dish. Combine sugar, milk, nutmeg, and cinnamon and stir to dissolve sugar. Add eggs and beat until mixture is well blended and smooth. Sprinkle raisins over donuts then pour egg mixture over both. Place in a preheated 350 degree oven and bake for 1 hour. Serve while warm or allow to cool, if desired.

*Adjust sugar to taste. 10-12 servings.

MISSOURI OFFERS VINTAGE **66** with plenty of sweeping curves and breathtaking views. The state has its own magic with plenty of byways waiting to be discovered. The Meramec Caverns area around Stanton offers great biker roads. Take it easy here, explore, tour the cave, then feast on a picnic in one of the nearby parks and unwind for awhile before venturing forth again. This potato salad makes for satisfying picnic fare.

Creamy New Potato Salad

1¼ pounds small red potatoes
1 cup plain low-fat yogurt
2 tablespoons Dijon mustard
2 tablespoons finely chopped fresh tarragon
½ small red pepper cut in matchstick strips
⅓ cup diced green onion
⅓ cup diagonally sliced celery
Salt and pepper to taste

Cook potatoes whole in boiling salted water until tender, about 25 minutes. Drain and cool. Cut potatoes into bite sized pieces.

Stir yogurt, mustard, and tarragon in large bowl until blended. Add potatoes, red pepper, onion, and

celery. Toss to blend. Season with salt and pepper to taste, cover, and chill before serving.
5-6 servings.

Meramec Caverns, Stanton

LOCATED IN THE LUXURIANT OZARK HERITAGE REGION in Missouri, both the Rosati Winery and the St. James Winery offer outstanding stops. These are great places for mailing gifts to jealous friends back home.

Sangria
ST. JAMES WINERY

1 bottle (750 ml) St. James Country Red Wine (or another good red wine)
1 orange, thinly sliced
1 lemon, thinly sliced
½ cup sugar
1 bottle (28 ounces) club soda

Combine the wine, orange, lemon, and sugar. Let sit one hour at room temperature. When ready to serve, add the club soda and serve over crushed ice. 6 eight-ounce servings.

WHEN YOU'RE BACK HOME AGAIN and still crave a taste of the Ozarks, here are a couple of dishes good enough to make you close your eyes and remember the pure adventure and freedom of Missouri. Great dishes don't have to have long, complicated names. This salad came straight from a Rolla garden and proves again that simple, wholesome dishes are hard to beat.

Wilted Greens with Country Ham

¼ cup olive oil
1 cup thinly sliced red onion
½ cup broken pecans
½ cup slivered country ham
2 tablespoons balsamic vinegar
2 tablespoons maple syrup

8 cups mixed fresh garden greens - kale, spinach, purple lettuce, arugula, cleaned and dry
Salt and pepper to taste

Heat olive oil in a large skillet. Add onions and saute, stirring constantly for about 5 minutes. Add nuts and continue cooking another two minutes. Stir in ham, continue cooking until ham is warm. Add vinegar and maple syrup. Stir and remove from heat.

Tear greens into a large bowl. Pour hot dressing over greens. Toss to wilt slightly. Sprinkle with salt and pepper to taste and serve immediately with crusty French bread. 8-10 servings.

Southern Baked Grits and Cheese

1½ cups grits
6 cups water
8 tablespoons butter or margarine
1 pound Velveeta cheese, cut into small chunks
1 teaspoon seasoned salt
3 eggs, well beaten
¼ teaspoon Tabasco sauce

Bring water to boil and add grits. Cook for 10 minutes or until thickened. Remove from heat and add 4 tablespoons of the butter or margarine, cheese, and salt. Stir until cheese is melted. Slowly add beaten eggs and Tabasco sauce. Melt remaining butter in a 9X12-inch baking dish. Pour grits mixture into the dish. Bake in a preheated 325 degree oven for 1 hour or until firm. 10 servings.

LEBANON'S MUNGER MOSS MOTEL IS A HIGHLIGHT for many bikers and biker tours. Trond Moberg calls the place "fantastic" and says he and his fellow Norwegian bikers always find a warm welcome from Bob and Ramona Lehman.

Munger Moss Motel, Lebanon

The name *Munger Moss* has a long history on Route 66. In 1947 Jesse and Pete Hudson bought the Chicken Shanty Cafe and some adjoining land in Lebanon. They changed the Chicken Shanty name to Munger Moss and built a motel next door. The cafe is gone now but Bob and Ramona continue to operate the motel that is one of the few mom-and-pop places along Route 66 with enough capacity to handle a large group of bikers.

Ramona shares this favorite salad recipe.

Ramona Lehman's Vegetable Salad

1 small head cauliflower, chopped
Equal amount of broccoli, chopped
1 bunch green onions, chopped
1 cup light salad dressing
⅓ cup sugar
2 tablespoons vinegar

Combine vegetables. Mix dressing ingredients and pour over vegetables. Toss, chill, and serve. 8-10 servings.

DOWN THE ROAD IN MARSHFIELD, home to Edwin Hubbell of space telescope fame, feast on barbecue at Tiny's Smokehouse. Then, when you're home again, feast on these pancakes often prepared at Marshfield's Dickey House while you reminisce about the trip.

Pumpkin Pancakes with Apple Cider Syrup
THE DICKEY HOUSE

1½ cups flour
1 teaspoon baking powder
¼ teaspoon baking soda
1½ teaspoons pumpkin pie spice
¼ teaspoon salt
1 egg
¼ cup canned pumpkin
1½ cups milk
3 tablespoons cooking oil

In a medium bowl, stir together the flour, baking powder, soda, salt, and pumpkin spice. In another bowl beat the egg, pumpkin, milk, and oil. Add milk mixture to the flour mixture and stir until just blended, but still lumpy. Pour about ¼ cup of batter for each pancake onto a hot griddle or heavy skillet. Cook over medium heat until browned, turning once to cook both sides. About 10 pancakes.

Apple Cider Syrup

½ cup sugar
4 teaspoons cornstarch
½ teaspoon cinnamon
1 cup apple cider or apple juice
1 tablespoon lemon juice
2 tablespoons butter or margarine

In a small saucepan stir together the sugar, cornstarch, and cinnamon. Add the apple cider and lemon juice. Cook for 2 minutes over medium heat until mixture is thickened and bubbly. Cook an additional 2 minutes. Remove from heat and stir in the butter or margarine. Serve while warm over pancakes. 1⅓ cups.

St. Louis

Lambert's Cafe

Lambert's Cafe, Home of the Throwed Rolls, was first opened in Sikeston, Missouri, in 1942 by Agnes and Earl Lambert. Their Springfield location has been open since March of 1994. Famous for good food and plenty of it, the owners began throwing rolls to their guests in 1976 and the tradition has continued. You'll never leave hungry here or go out without a few laughs. A real Ozark welcome awaits. Lambert's is 7 miles south of Springfield on Highway 65.

CASHEW CHICKEN IS A COMMUNITY TRADITION in Springfield. It was first prepared at several outstanding Chinese restaurants in the area and is now considered a community classic and a cherished symbol of the city. There are a number of similar versions. This one comes from Tommy and Glenda Pike and their daughter, Tonya. Tommy is the current president of the Missouri Route 66 Association.

Springfield Cashew Chicken

2 large boneless chicken breast halves, cut into about 10 bite sized chunks

Marinade:
3 tablespoons sherry (or water)
½ teaspoon Accent Seasoning
1 teaspoon sugar
1 tablespoon oyster sauce
Dash of ginger
Dash of garlic powder
1 teaspoon salt
½ teaspoon pepper

Combine marinade ingredients and pour over chicken pieces. Allow to stand in refrigerator several hours but overnight is preferable. If chicken breasts are extra large, double the marinade recipe. When ready to cook, drain the chicken well and dispose of marinade.

To Fry:
¼ cup milk
¼ cup water
4 tablespoons cornstarch, divided
2 large eggs, beaten
Peanut oil for frying

Combine the milk, water, and 1 tablespoon of the cornstarch. Blend until smooth. Gradually stir in eggs and continue beating until mixture is smooth. Dip chicken in remaining cornstarch, then in egg mixture. Deep fry the chicken in hot oil (about 375 degrees) until done. Drain and keep warm.

Sauce:
1 chicken bouillon cube
1 cup water
1½ tablespoon cornstarch
1 teaspoon sugar
½ teaspoon Accent Seasoning
1 tablespoon oyster sauce
¼ teaspoon ginger
Dash of garlic powder
¼ teaspoon salt
¼ cup water

Heat bouillon cube in hot water to dissolve, then allow to cool slightly. While cooling, mix together the remaining ingredients. Add mixture to the cooled bouillon and heat until mixture is thick and clear.

To serve:
Rice
⅓ cup cashew nuts
¼ cup chopped onions
Soy sauce

Cook rice according to package directions, preparing enough for 3-4 cups of cooked rice. Arrange rice on a platter and top with chicken. Pour the sauce over the chicken and top with cashew nuts. Sprinkle with chopped green onions. Serve soy sauce on the side. Serve while warm. 2 servings.

LEAVE SPRINGFIELD ON ROUTE 66 and drive the original alignment all the way to Oklahoma City, one of the longest undisturbed segments along the road.

In Halltown, stop to admire Whitehall Mercantile, operated by Jerry and Thelma White, in the oldest building still standing. The town was once the busiest antique center along Route 66. Several shops still remain open along here. Matthias Guenther, a Harley rider from Germany, found an antique dealer advertising free coffee and discovered a bonus of friendly conversation and several pieces of old German music. "And the coffee was really free," he remembers.

Christina Hey and Matthias Guenther at a Halltown antique shop

Thelma White's Sour Cream Raisin Pie

1⅓ cups sugar
1½ tablespoons flour
⅔ teaspoon nutmeg
⅔ teaspoon cinnamon
Pinch of salt
3 eggs, lightly beaten
2 cups sour cream
2 cups raisins

Combine dry ingredients and add lightly beaten eggs. Stir in sour cream and raisins. Pour mixture into two unbaked pie shells. Bake in preheated 425 degree oven for 20 minutes then reduce heat to 375 and continue baking for another 30 minutes. Two 9-inch pies.

Ever Dream of Ghosts?

Between Halltown and Carthage, there's plenty of opportunity to find a few as you ramble past a dozen or so long-gone remains of 66 communities with fanciful names like Paris Springs, Heatonville, Albatross, Phelps, Rescue, Plew, Avilla, and Maxville. Every state along 66 has its share of ghost towns, but the skeletons along here come less than five miles apart and remind bikers what it must have been like when a constant stream of folks helped support the gas stations, greasy spoons, and imaginings of countless dreamers. When did these folks move on, where did they go, and who did they leave behind around these abandoned rock walls?

JUST BEFORE YOU ENTER CARTHAGE, VEER NORTH to Lowell Davis's *Red Oak II*. Lowell is retired now, so his forty-acre farm and amazing recreated village of Red Oak II has new caretakers. The complex is often open. Take a drive through this labyrinth of Lowell's genius, hand-crafted from his fertile imagination. There are over a dozen restored buildings, including a Phillips 66 Station, a feed and seed store, Grandpa Weber's Blacksmith, the Salem County church, even a recreation of the original home of Belle Starr's family. Take a look at Sparrowville, his airplane made from pipe, and his huge faucet sculpture. This is a place you are guaranteed to remember!

Here is a caramel corn recipe very similar to the one passed down by Lowell's mom, Nell Davis.

Red Oak II Caramel Corn

7 quarts popped corn
2 cups brown sugar
2 sticks margarine
½ cup white corn syrup
½ teaspoon salt
½ teaspoon vanilla
½ teaspoon soda

Place popped corn in a large oven-proof container. Combine brown sugar, margarine, corn syrup, and salt in sauce pan. Boil five minutes. Stir in vanilla and soda. Pour immediately over the popped corn. Stir and place in a 250 degree oven for one hour, stirring every 15 minutes. Add peanuts, if desired. Cool and enjoy.

IN NEARBY JOPLIN, FRED AND RED'S on South Main has served up some of the best chili and spaghetti in the area for years. Lea Ona Essley, from nearby Baxter Springs shared this spaghetti topping that is very close to the original recipe at Fred and Red's. She says the secret ingredient is the addition of tamales to the sauce which adds both body and flavor.

Fred and Red's Chili

1 large (28-ounce) can tamales, mashed
1 pound cooked hamburger
½ cup chopped onion
Water to make a thick sauce
1 (8-ounce) can tomato sauce
1 (1-ounce package) Williams Chili Seasoning Mix
1 pound brick chili

Mash the tamales. Cook the hamburger and drain; add onion and mashed tamales, then enough water to make a sauce. Add tomato sauce, chili seasoning, and brick chili and heat to boiling. Reduce heat and simmer for 10 minutes. Note: Serve this chili plain or as a sauce over pasta. Approximately 9 cups.

YOU'LL FIND NO BARRIERS TO FREEDOM along this stretch of the road but you may want to slow down around the historic State Line Bar before heading toward that short but rich slice of Route 66 in Kansas. ∎

The Chain of Rocks Bridge near St. Louis

Lost In America

— MICHAEL WALLIS

Visitors from abroad are one of the fastest growing categories of Route 66 travelers. Each year more and more people eager to traverse the Mother Road come to America from Japan, New Zealand, Australia, Canada, Brazil, France, the United Kingdom, Norway, Belgium, and Germany.

They come in tour groups and pack into big comfortable buses or they rent cars and take to the old road. Still others want to do the trip right — on the back of a motorcycle. They either rent bikes in Chicago or L.A., or else ship their own scooters to one of the old road's terminal cities for their journey of a lifetime.

Nina and Camillo Pinto, riders from Portugal, on Route 66, St. Louis

It seems many of the foreign visitors I encounter on Route 66 come from Germany which makes sense since Germans are among the world's most frequent travelers. I remember a quartet of young German professionals I met on the old road. They were all on their Harleys shipped from Germany and they were making the westward journey on Route 66 from Chicago to Santa Monica. We swapped road yarns and one of them told me why he made the long trip.

"We are seeing the best of America," Uwe Langner, the unofficial group leader, told me. "This is what we came for — the wind, the sand, the mountains, the great distances. And, then the people — we can now see that the people on Route 66 are a big family. They are so real."

For Uwe, a policeman back in Germany, the cycle odyssey was a dream come true. Since he first saw the motion picture, "Easy Rider," he has longed to come to the United States and traverse Route 66. On his well-worn helmet was an America flag he painted himself almost thirty years past. "Riding Route 66 is special," he said with emotion in his voice, "but riding this road on my Harley is extra special."

Of course, I had to agree.

And then I considered a pair of German bikers I met during a Harley cruise of Route 66 some years past. They, too, were respectable middle age professionals — classic "Rich Urban Bikers" (RUBS), only German.

Up state in Illinois I told them how to negotiate the various alignments of Route 66 making its way through St. Louis. I gave them some directions and advice but despite this they ended up hopelessly lost in city traffic and well off the route. To add to their misery it started raining and nightfall was approaching.

Unsure of just what to do, they pulled up to an intersection stop light and one of the bikers tapped on the driver's window of a black limousine stopped in the next lane. The driver, apparently frightened of a biker decked out in leather and goggles, did not respond.

Then the back window went down and the bikers saw a distinguished gentleman dressed in a tuxedo and next to him his lovely lady also dressed to the nines. The man was smiling and he asked the bikers if they were riding Harleys. They said they were and when the man heard their strong accents he asked if they were from Germany. They said yes and they told him they were lost and were just trying to find shelter for the night. The man told them to follow his limo. They did as they were told.

The bikers dutifully tagged along as the limo made its way through evening traffic. It finally pulled into the circular drive at the elegant Ritz-Carlton Hotel and stopped beneath the canopy at the main entrance. The Germans were alarmed. They knew their travel budget did not allow for such extravagant lodging and besides they were just a couple of dirty, wet, and dog-tired bikers who did not fit the hotel's clientele profile.

Before the Germans could take their leave, the gentleman was out of the limo with his wife. He gave the driver some instructions and then told the bikers they would be his guests for the evening. He would not listen to their polite protests and, with the wet riders in tow, the foursome entered the hotel. They proceeded to a magnificent ballroom filled with people in formal clothes seated at tables decked out in fine linen and covered with fancy china and silver.

The gentleman led his party to a main table and told a hovering waiter to make room for his unexpected guests. He had another waiter take them to the men's room to freshen up and when they returned they were seated next to the man and his wife.

It seems this gentleman was the guest of honor at his gala retirement party. He also was a motorcycle fan and had always wanted to take one out on the open road. That was his dream.

When the Germans turned down offers of champagne their host asked what they desired and then had frosty glasses of beer brought to the table. There were toasts all around and by the end of the evening the bikers were the talk of the party, especially among the tittering ladies. Following dinner the Germans were told that a suite awaited them, again compliments of the gentleman.

A day or so later, when I bumped into the Germans out on Route 66 as it makes its way through the Ozarks, they eagerly told me of their adventure. No matter what waited for them down the road, they already knew that Missouri was their favorite state on Route 66.

I have always thought that it is good to get lost when traveling the old road. It can be worrisome but it can also lead to unexpected pleasures. Cruising Route 66 should be a scavenger hunt. Just remember that the treasure the road has to offer is not always gold or silver. Sometimes it is better.* ∎

---

* It is unknown if the mysterious gentleman host ever got his Harley.

Building of 66

— MICHAEL WALLIS

Route 66 was not built in a day. It took years of planning, cajoling, and heated debate to create the highway that would span two-thirds of the continent through eight states, several major cities, and three time zones.

Americans were anxious to get better roads. That desire developed into a full-fledged movement as the Twenties roared and automobiles became affordable thanks to mass production. Everyday folks took to existing roads in their new cars. As they explored further from home, the need for a highway system to link the country became apparent.

Private road clubs and associations of highway officials formed. Legislation was passed calling for road construction. In Oklahoma, Cyrus Stevens Avery and his cohorts pushed for a federal highway to connect Chicago and Santa Monica. Shortly after the highway was christened in 1926, Cy Avery became forever known as "The Father of Route 66."

At first only 800 miles of the route was paved. It took until 1937 to pave the rest. But the inconvenience of patchwork road and interruptions of thick mud didn't stop motorists and motorcyclists from taking to the road in numbers so great that Route 66 soon became known as the Main Street of America. ∎

Kansas

Fast facts from Kansas

- Cross the state on Route 66 in only 13.2 miles.

- The first state to pave all of Route 66.

- Baxter Springs residents boast their city was the "first cowtown in Kansas."

- A half-marathon run from Oklahoma to Missouri is often on the calendar when fall weather arrives.

Kansas Biker Road Rules

- Safety Helmet, required by law under age of 18

- Eye Protection, required by law unless equipped with windscreen

Must see in Kansas

- GALENA — Katy Depot and Galena Mining and Historical Museum

- WEST MINERAL — Drive north on Highway 69 to see the second largest electrical shovel in the world — Big Brutus — sixteen stories high and 5,500 tons.

- RIVERTON — Concrete truss "Rainbow" bridge — Built in the 20s between Riverton and Baxter Springs

- BAXTER SPRINGS — Heritage Center & Historical Museum

Rainbow Curve Bridge, Baxter Springs

Favorite hangouts for food and drink

- GALENA

UP IN SMOKE — new to the road but destined to become a favorite stop, Roger Wormington has opened a barbecue pit in an old gas station/barber shop at 418 S. Main. An old train engine sits next to the smoker and the aroma of tasty meat wafts through the neighborhood.

- Riverton

EISLER BROTHERS OLD RIVERTON STORE, built in 1925 and still a real working general store, it is operated by Scott Nelson, president of the Kansas Historic Route 66 Association. Some of the best sandwiches on the road can be found here — made fresh at the old-fashioned deli and served with cold soda.

The Sunflower State

KANSAS

Topeka ★

66

Baxter Springs ⊙

- Baxter Springs
  - CAFE ON THE ROUTE AND LITTLE BRICK INN (upstairs), 1101 Military Ave. "The restaurant in the bank that was robbed by Jesse James." Formerly was Bill Murphey's Restaurant, famous for pies since 1941.
  - MURPHEY'S RESTAURANT
    1046 Military Ave.
    Now located in the old Baxter National Bank building diagonally across the street from 1101 Military.

Eisler Brothers Old Riverton Store, Riverton

Outlaw Bikers

—MICHAEL WALLIS

When you are out on Route 66 nothing is predictable. That is why so many bikers like traveling the old road. There is a sense of excitement and motion and the possibility for pure adventure around every curve and bend.

Every facet of humanity can be found on Route 66 — bluebloods and rednecks, the godless and Jesus freaks, filthy rich and dirt poor, card-carrying members of the NRA as well as the ACLU. There have been both a Ralph Lauren and a K-Mart line of Route 66 clothing. This diversity is one of the many reasons Harley riders fit right in on America's Main Street.

Today's bikers — just like the highway they love — cross all demographic lines. When you attend a rally or participate in an organized tour, your fellow bikers may include dentists, lawyers, rabbis, and poets, or plumbers, mechanics, steelworkers, and truckers. It doesn't matter a wit.

I have journeyed on Route 66 with federal judges and ex-cons at the same time and never even knew it until long after our ride had ended. That is because we seldom discuss a man or woman's profession or their net worth. All we are interested in is our ride. We care about that moment out on a stretch of highway where we can be who we want to be and nobody gives a damn.

Many of the old guard bikers — especially the guys carrying chain wallets who sported tattoos long before housewives and college kids started getting them —

Galena

don't much care for "Rich Urban Bikers," or RUBs. I keep friends in each of the camps and enjoy the company of both on Route 66 trips.

Some years ago, I recall riding with some RUBs and also a few old guards along the 13.2 miles of vintage Mother Road that just nips the southeastern corner of Kansas.

As we scooted down the road making cold drink and beef jerky stops in the towns of Galena and then Riverton, I thought about how this particular stretch of Route 66 had served as a good bootlegger road during the dry times when the highway was brand new. I recalled colorful tales about mysterious automobiles sneaking out of Joplin to the east; their trunks loaded with illicit hootch to quench the thirst of folks in Kansas and Oklahoma.

Route 66 — a truly democratic highway — boasts a rich outlaw legacy. Stories of felons and their ilk are forever entwined in the history of the highway through all eight states. Long before Route 66 was ever thought about, the trails and paths that eventually became the highway were frequented by all sorts of mounted bandits and killers including Billy the Kid, Belle Starr, the James Gang, Henry Starr, and the Daltons.

Then after Route 66 was officially created in 1926, a new breed of desperado took to the road. The list includes Al Capone and his gangster buddies in Chicago and Cicero and an array of other Depression-era criminals such as "Charles "Pretty Boy" Floyd, Bonnie Parker and Clyde Barrow, George "Machine Gun" Kelly, and Ma Barker and her brood of wicked sons.

With all that in mind, when my diverse gang of bikers pulled in for gas on the edge of Riverton, I pulled out some of my better outlaw memories. I told them about the 1863 Baxter Springs Massacre when the notorious Confederate guerrilla William Quantrill attacked and killed a small force of Union soldiers. I also talked of other infamous villains who had left their marks right where we headed — Baxter Springs, still proudly called "The First Cow Town in Kansas." That got everybody's attention.

Baxter Springs

We fired up the bikes and rolled out onto the road. Immediately I sensed my fellow riders' excitement. Only a short time later, as we approached Baxter Springs, my imagination got the best of me. I pretended that we were no longer modern-day bikers but instead we had become steel-jawed brigands. Our bikes changed into cow ponies, our helmets were transformed into black hats, and our leather jackets turned into long linen dusters like the old-time outlaws often wore. The voice of Tex Ritter singing "High Noon" echoed in my head.

Baxter Springs

Rolling slowly into downtown Baxter Springs we scanned the sidewalks and shop windows for any high sheriffs or tin star deputies. We parked our bikes in front of a two-story brick edifice with striped awnings shading the windows and a brick wall adorned with a mural and the words Cafe on the Route. Ironically it was high noon but even "outlaws" have to eat, and besides, there was no sign of Gary Cooper.

Once inside and comfortably seated at a long table, I continued to regale my gang with more stories while we waited for our meals to be served. I spoke of elderly citizens who remembered the October afternoon in 1933 when Wilbur Underhill — the notorious "Tri-State Terror" — robbed the American Bank in Baxter Springs. The old timers also recollected that "Pretty Boy" Floyd gassed up regularly at Spencer's Shell Station when he came this way. And they had bitter memories of Bonnie

and Clyde in 1933 when they robbed the Baxter Springs General Store twice in one month. Then the following year the crazed couple, on a murderous rampage, shot and killed a policeman just down the highway in nearby Commerce, Oklahoma.

I paused for a time when our food came steaming from the kitchen on big trays — mostly cowboy steaks smothered in fried tobacco onions, roast beef hash, and piles of corn muffins. And for me — a full rack of barbecued pork spareribs drenched with strawberry sauce and festooned with fresh strawberries the size of a baby's fist.

For dessert, I finished my outlaw lecture by pointing out that just across the street from where we sat gorged to the gills was Murphey's Restaurant. Renowned for superb pies, Murphey's is in a building that once housed the National Bank of Baxter Springs. There in 1914 the legendary Henry Starr, whose criminal career spanned more than 32 years, made a sizable and unauthorized cash withdrawal.

Before the other bikers could vacate the cafe to check out Murphey's, I stopped them in their tracks. I had saved the best for last. Over toothpicks and coffee, I explained that for many years Murphey's was located in the building where we had just dined, now occupied by the Cafe on the Route and an upstairs bed and breakfast. But way back in 1870 when it was erected, the building was known as the Crowell Bank, the first banking establishment in town.

Murphey's Restaurant, in the old National Bank of Baxter Springs building

Michael Wallis tackles lunch fit for an outlaw, Baxter Springs

In 1876, Jesse James and Cole Younger — two of the best-known outlaws in America — rode into Baxter Springs, tied their horses to a corncrib, and strolled into the bank. They pulled their guns and fled with $2,900. The outlaws rode out of town on what is now Route 66, disarmed a pursuing posse without firing a single shot, and made good their escape to Indian Territory, now called Oklahoma.

I proposed we do the same — head for old Indian Territory — only without the robbery part. We settled up our food bill and within 10 minutes we were out of Kansas and in the Sooner State.

All the rest of the day we made our way to Tulsa, digesting that tasty lunch along with those rich stories from long ago. ■

Get Your Kicks

— MICHAEL WALLIS

Many people say Route 66 is the most famous highway in the United States. I agree. Others claim it may be the best known highway in the world. I won't argue with them either. From Chicago to Santa Monica the Route 66 signs are returning to help show the way as we make the best kind of neon journey along this passageway of memory that helped shape our country's history and culture.

That is what a Route 66 odyssey is all about. Especially for bikers. It is the most special trip you may ever take — down America's Main Street that is sure to rekindle memories and spark your curiosity.

Remember this always — life truly does begin on the off-ramp. By merely daring to exit the interstate highway, you can climb onto Route 66 and discover storytellers, secret corners, and hidden towns. Just cruise the open road to the tune of your humming motor, open your eyes to the possibilities and maybe, just maybe, discover something of yourself.

Recipes from Kansas (and Norway)

— MARIAN CLARK

Trond Moberg's caravan of Norwegian bikers cruise Route 66 three to four times every year. The group averages thirty bikes and about fifty bikers. Trond says one of his group's favorite stops is at Eisler Brothers Old Riverton Store where they are always welcome. He swears Scott Nelson makes the best sandwiches on Route 66. Scott modestly says the sandwiches are good because they are always made individually from fresh ingredients and "like we would make them to eat ourselves." It also helps when Scott wears his Norwegian T-shirt as he helps to create the masterpieces behind the old-fashioned meat counter. During a recent stop by the Norwegian group, Scott invited a friend and his Norwegian-born father to the feast. It was hard to tell who had the best time as they shared experiences in their own language with gusto.

Trond shared these recipes that he often uses when bikers meet in Norway to plan their Route 66 trips.

Cold Poached Salmon

6 salmon cutlets, approximately 1½ inches thick
Poach in 2 quarts of water with:
1 lemon, sliced
10-12 whole peppercorns
1 bay leaf
1 sprig of fresh dill
1¼ teaspoons salt

Poach the salmon for approximately 15 minutes. Remove from heat and allow the salmon to cool in the water. Serve at room temperature with boiled potatoes, sour cream, and cucumber salad. 6 servings

Cucumber Salad

1 cucumber, thinly sliced
¼ cup apple cider vinegar
6 tablespoons white sugar
Salt and pepper to taste

Combine and serve at room temperature.

Lamb and Cabbage Stew

2 pounds lamb shoulder, cut into serving pieces
2 pounds white cabbage
4 teaspoons black peppercorns
1 tablespoon salt
2 cups boiling water

Place meat and cabbage in layers in pan, starting with lamb, finishing with a top layer of cabbage. Sprinkle each layer with salt and pepper. Add boiling water, cover and simmer for about 1½ hours without removing the lid. Serve with boiled potatoes. 4 servings.

BAXTER SPRINGS IS QUIET NOW but was a boomtown during the days of the great cattle drives. Today it's a place to experience America as it was in the past. Nothing reflects great all-American food better than banana bread — this Kansas version is easy and satisfying!

NORWEGIAN

ROUTE

66

tours

40 grader Celcius

tre tidssoner

kameratskap

spenning

prærie

opplevelse

USA

La dine drømmer
bli virkelighet!

samhold

Chicago

åtte stater

4000 km

Harley-Davidson

ørken

Canyon

Banana Bread

2 medium-sized bananas
1 apple, chopped
1 egg
¼ cup butter or margarine
1 cup sugar
2 cups flour
1 teaspoon baking soda

Combine banana, apple, egg, butter, and sugar in a food processor. Pulse until smooth. Add flour and baking soda. Pulse to moisten. Turn into a greased 8 ½ x 4½-inch bread pan. Bake in a preheated 350 degree oven for 1 hour.

WHILE MARY ELLEN LEE RAN THE LOTTIE KEENAN HOUSE in Baxter Springs, locals said her cinnamon rolls were some of the best ever. Cinnamon rolls rank right up there with chicken-fried steak and pecan pie as mouth-watering road food. Try Mary Ellen's version and you'll agree.

Cinnamon Roll Muffins

LOTTIE KEENAN HOUSE

2 packages dry yeast
¼ cup warm water
1 cup lukewarm milk
1 cup margarine, melted
2 eggs, beaten
¼ cup sugar
1 teaspoon salt
4 ½ cups flour

Filling:

2 sticks softened margarine
sugar and cinnamon, as desired

Dissolve yeast in warm water. Combine yeast mixture with remaining ingredients, in order given, in a large mixing bowl. Beat until smooth, about one minute. Dough will be very soft. Cover with a damp cloth and place in refrigerator overnight.

The next morning roll out half the dough into a rectangle and spread with one stick of softened margarine. Sprinkle dough with desired amount of sugar and cinnamon. Roll dough from long side in jelly-roll fashion. Cut dough into 1½ inch slices and place cut side down into greased muffin tins. Repeat process for remaining half of dough. Bake cinnamon rolls in preheated 350 degree oven for about 25 minutes. Cool and glaze with a powdered sugar icing, if desired. About 2 dozen cinnamon rolls.

"BURNT OFFERINGS" WAS A POPULAR WEEKLY FOOD COLUMN that appeared in the *Baxter Springs Citizen* for many years. Carolyn Nichols, who compiled the articles, is a long time Baxter Springs resident whose father started the paper.

Carolyn shared her recipe for watermelon pickles because she says the men in her family in particular are fans. Old-fashioned watermelon pickles are best when made with the thick white rind from dark green Black Diamond melons. Mmmm, what a wonderful old-fashioned treat!

Carolyn Nichols' Watermelon Pickles

6 pounds watermelon rind (about half a large melon)

Cut pink meat and green rind from white. Cut white rind into 1-inch squares, or whatever shape you prefer. Cover rind with cold salted water. Do not use iodized salt. Soak overnight. The next morning, drain and rinse melon pieces thoroughly. Cook in clear water until rind is fork tender, but don't overcook. Drain well.

Make a syrup of:

8 cups sugar
1⅔ cups any cider vinegar
4 drops oil of cloves
6 drops oil of cinnamon
A few drops of green coloring (optional)

Boil syrup for 5 minutes. Add rind and let stand overnight. The next morning add 1 cup sugar and bring to a boil. Can in hot sterilized jars. If any syrup is left, save for another batch. It will keep for two weeks in refrigerator. Makes 4 pints per 6 pounds of melon rind.

SHIRLEY ELLSWORTH SHARED THIS CANDY RECIPE that was first made at Anthony's Candy Store in Galena. Called Mine Run Candy, many thought Mr. Anthony gave it this name because the crisp porous texture reminded him of the minerals that were mined in the area. But he always claimed that it came about as an accident, when he allowed some candy to caramelize while he wasn't paying attention and "let his mind run wild." Whatever the reason, Mine Run Candy is a local favorite.

Mine Run Candy

1 cup sugar
1 cup dark corn syrup
1 tablespoon white vinegar
1 tablespoon soda

Combine sugar, syrup, and vinegar in a large pan and cook, stirring constantly until sugar dissolves. Cover pan for one minute to wash down crystals.

Uncover pan, insert candy thermometer, and cook candy without stirring to 300 degrees, or the hard-crack stage. Remove from heat and stir in soda. Candy will foam so be sure to use a large pan and a big spoon with a long handle.

Pour mixture into a buttered 9x13-inch dish. Do not spread. After it cools, break into bite sized pieces and coat with chocolate.

Chocolate Coating:

Melt a block of almond bark or dark chocolate for about 90 seconds in a microwave. Watch carefully and don't overcook. Dip the candy pieces into the melted chocolate and set on waxed paper to cool. ■

Grapes of Wrath

— MICHAEL WALLIS

Route 66 has endured several incarnations, including the bittersweet 1930s when the nation's economy cracked and the rains stopped, bringing drought and destruction to America's heartland.

I grew up hearing stories of those tragic years that left indelible scars on the land and the people along the highway. Large parts of Oklahoma, Texas, Kansas, and Arkansas looked like moonscape after huge black clouds swept across fields and towns.

A great migration resulted. Tens of thousands of Okies, Arkies, tenant farmers, disenfranchised workers, vagabonds, and migrants turned to the highway. They fled the choking dust and desolation and headed west to rebuild shattered dreams and start new lives in California.

Route 66 became a road of safe passage to the Promised Land. Woody Guthrie crafted his most poignant ballads. John Steinbeck gave the highway yet another name — the Mother Road — in his immortal novel, *The Grapes of Wrath*.

When those pilgrims reached the steep mountain grades in Arizona and looked down at the Colorado River and toward the golden land just beyond, called California, they became euphoric. They were a lost tribe, but they could almost smell the sweet orange blossoms, the sea air, and the fertile soil waiting just ahead.

Oklahoma

Fast facts from Oklahoma

- Approximate Route 66 mileage in Oklahoma — 394
- Oklahoma is the only state with oil rigs on the state capital lawn.
- Tulsa is home to Cyrus Avery, "The Father of Route 66."
- The state flower is the mistletoe, the state animal is the bison, and the state fish is the white bass.

Oklahoma Biker Road Rules

- Safety Helmet, required by law under age 18
- Eye Protection, required by law unless equipped with windscreen

Where to Buy Stuff in Oklahoma

- *TULSA* — Lyon's Indian Store, 401 East 11th Street (Route 66)
- *WELLSTON* — Seaba Station, one mile east of Hwy. 177 on Route 66
- *ARCADIA* — Round Barn, on old Route 66
- *CLINTON* — Oklahoma Route 66 Museum, 2229 W. Gary, Route 66

Must see in Oklahoma

- *QUAPAW* — Spook Light on Devil's Promenade Road, east of town
- *COMMERCE* — Baseball enthusiast? See Mickey Mantle's home at 319 S. Quincy.
- *MIAMI* — Coleman Theater, 103 N. Main, built in 1929 — Spanish Mission style
- *RIBBON ROAD* — Two stretches of original nine-feet-wide road between Miami and Afton
- *AFTON* — Restored DX gas station rest stop, run by Laurel Kane

The Sooner State

OKLAHOMA

Oklahoma City ★ — 66 — ⊙ Tulsa

- *VINITA*
  - The oldest Oklahoma town on Route 66, founded in 1871
  - Summerside Vineyards, Winery & Inn, I-44 & Historic Route 66
  - America's largest McDonalds in square footage, built as the Glass House in 1958, spans I-44 near Vinita.

- *BIG CABIN* — Cabin Creek Vineyards. Turn south from Route 66 at State Highway 69 and follow the signs or take Exit 283 on I-44.

Ed Galloway's Totem Poles, Foyil

- *FOYIL*
  - Ed Galloway's Totem Poles, east on State Highway 28A; one of the best examples of folk art in the country
  - Monument to favorite son Andy Payne, winner of the 1928 Bunion Derby that earned him $25,000 to help pay off his family farm

- *CLAREMORE*
  - Will Rogers Memorial Museum and Tomb, 1720 West Will Rogers Boulevard
  - Will Rogers' Birthplace, the Dogiron Ranch, off Highway 88 between Claremore and Oologah
  - J.M. Davis Gun Museum, 333 N. Lynn Riggs, the largest one-man collection in the world

- *CATOOSA* — Blue Whale Theme Park

- *TULSA*
  - 11th Street, Cyrus Avery Route 66 Memorial Bridge across the Arkansas River
  - Cain's Ballroom, 423 N. Main St., an icon of Western Swing music. Bob Wills and the Texas Playboys performed on KVOO radio from here for nine years. Recently restored.
  - Discoveryland, 19501 W. 41 Street, 5 miles west of State Hwy 93 (Sand Springs). Summertime outdoor live performances of Oklahoma!

- SAPULPA — Mr. Indian Cowboy Store, 1000 S. Main, Native American owned and operated

- BRISTOW — More brick-paved streets than any other Oklahoma community. There's a different feel here.

- CHANDLER — Restored Phillips 66 Service Station

- ARCADIA — Round Barn, built in 1898 from native Burr Oak.

- OKLAHOMA CITY
  - Oklahoma State Capital Complex, NE 23rd and Lincoln, call 521-3356. The only state capitol with working oil wells located on the grounds
  - Remington Park Race Track, 1 Remington Pl. World class pari-mutuel horseracing
  - Milk bottle building, 25th and Classen, across from Kamp's Grocery
  - Bricktown Historical District. Revitalized warehouse district with good restaurants and night spots

Bikers paying respects at site of Murrah Building, Oklahoma City

- YUKON — Sign atop Yukon Flour Mill can be seen for miles at night. The mill operated from 1900 until 1970.

- Hydro — Lucille Hamon's Gas Station (now closed), Route 66, north access road of I-40

- WEATHERFORD
  - Astronaut Thomas Stafford NASA Museum, located at the airport, northeast of town
  - Cotter Blacksmith and Machine Shop, 208 W. Rainey. Family operated since 1913

- CLINTON — Oklahoma Route 66 Museum, 2229 W. Gary Boulevard, (Exit 65 from I-40)

Route 66 Museum, Clinton

- ELK CITY — National Route 66 Museum, Route 66 and Pioneer Road, a part of Old Town Museum Complex

Bikers at groundbreaking for National Route 66 Museum, Elk City

- SAYRE — Steel Truss bridge, near Exit 26 from I-40 and once a part of Route 66

Sayre

- ERICK
  - Honey Farm, two miles west and a mile north
  - Sand Hills Curiosity Shop (formerly City Meat Market). A favorite biker stop owned by Harley and Annabelle Russell. "The Redneck Capitol of the World"

In front of the Sand Hills Curiosity Shop, Erick

- TEXOLA
  - Old Territorial Jail, one block north of Route 66 on Main. No windows or doors on this building.
  - Last Stop Bar. Check out the sign.

Beacons in the dark

- Chandler — Lincoln Motel, 740 East 1st Street. A return to 1939 when this Route 66 motor court was built

- Arcadia — Hillbillee's Bed and Breakfast, 206 East Highway 66. Rebuilt from a Route 66 log motor court by Wade and Norma Braxton. Several rooms have been carefully restored as a bed and breakfast. A regular biker stop

- Clinton — Best Western Trade Winds Courtyard Inn, 2128 Gary Blvd., across street from Oklahoma Route 66 Museum

- Sayre — Old Hotel, 311 West Main

Favorite hangouts for food and drink

- MIAMI
  - PIZZA HUT EXPRESS, 101 A Street NW, behind Coleman Theater
  - WAYLAN'S KU-KU BURGER, 915 N. Main, a great place for a hamburger

- VINITA
  - CLANTON'S CAFE, 319 E. Illinois, a four-generation Route 66 eatery

- FOYIL
  - TOP HAT DAIRY BAR, Crossroads of Highway 66 and 28A. A biker-friendly place filled with memorabilia.

- CLAREMORE
  - HAMMETT HOUSE, 1616 West Will Rogers Boulevard, long-time local favorite
  - COTTON EYED JOE'S BARBECUE, 715 Moretz. Mighty good food here!

- TULSA
  - METRO DINER, 3001 East 11th, Route 66. Fifties decor, neon, 66 roadhouse atmosphere
  - WEBER'S GRILL, 3801 S. Peoria. Credited with inventing the hamburger by owners Harold and Rick Bilby, who say their great-grandfather was serving burgers in Indian Territory in 1891. Weber's Root Beer is also a classic.

- OLLIE'S STATION RESTAURANT, 4070 Southwest Blvd. (Route 66). Train buffs love this place with its hometown atmosphere.
- CROW CREEK TAVERN, 3435 S. Peoria, a popular biker stop in the Brookside area
- TALLY'S GOOD FOOD CAFE, 1102 South Yale
- CORNER CAFE, 1103 South Peoria
- ROUTE 66 DINER, 313 East 2nd Street, on the original alignment across the street from the Blue Dome Gas Station

- *Bristow* — ANCHOR DRIVE IN, 630 S. Roland. A family-run hamburger and barbecue stop on Route 66 since the late 1940s

- *Stroud* — ROCK CAFE, 114 West Main. Opened August 4, 1939, a Route 66 classic

- *Davenport* — DAN'S BARBECUE PIT, rated as one of the ten best barbecue outposts in the country by Rich Davis, creator of K.C. Masterpiece barbecue sauce

- *Chandler* — GRANNY'S COUNTRY KITCHEN, 917 Manvel. Old fashioned country breakfasts and blue plate specials

- *Arcadia* — HILLBILLEE'S CAFE — A favorite biker stop. Features pecan smoked barbecue, chicken fried steak, and classic hamburgers with fries. Live music regularly

- *OKLAHOMA CITY*
  - THE COUNTY LINE RESTAURANT, 1226 NE 63rd. Built before the depression and known for years as the Kentucky Club, this is truly a restaurant with a past.
  - ANN'S CHICKEN FRY, 4106 NW 39th. Great Route 66 decor inside and out, plus chicken fried steak and fried peaches
  - BEVERLY'S PANCAKE CORNER, 2115 NW Expressway. The final resting place for the famous "Chicken in the Rough" chain, an OKC legend
  - MEIKI'S ROUTE 66 RESTAURANT, 4533 NW 39th. Route 66 decor, Italian food

- *YUKON* — SID'S DINER, 4 East Main

- *EL RENO*
  - JOHNNIE'S GRILL, 301 S. Rock Island. Try onion fried burgers.
  - SID'S DINER, 300 S. Chocktaw

- *ELK CITY*
  - COUNTRY DOVE GIFTS AND TEA ROOM, 610 W. 3rd, for the best lunch in town.
  - JIGGS SMOKE HOUSE, Parkersberg Road Exit from I-40

- *Erick* — RAFTER T RESTAURANT (formerly Cal's Country Cooking), I-40 at Exit 7

Lone rider cruises the "Pony" bridge near Bridgeport

Why the Motorcycle Keeps Boys on the Farm

Beneath this bold headline, a clever Harley sales pitch in the Oklahoma Farm Journal of June 15, 1913 surely must have attracted its fair share of new cycle riders. This advertisement appeared just six years after statehood and 13 years before Route 66 was officially created.

"Don't expect your boy to be happy on the farm if the summer season brings only work. When the day's work is over don't tell him the horses are too tired for road work, because it is this tying to the farm, this inability to join his chums in their pastimes or to seek his own pleasures that often makes farm life distasteful to him. Get him a *HARLEY-DAVIDSON*. It will let down the bars and take him where he wishes in a fraction of the time he would use by team. It will open up a thousand and one pleasures heretofore denied him. You will find he will return at bedtime, happy, contented and satisfied with his lot in life." ∎

The Rock

— MICHAEL WALLIS

It's Saturday morning in Tulsa, Oklahoma, and I have nothing but open Mother Road ahead of me. I pull on fresh jeans and leathers and declare myself ready to take on the day.

My sweet Harley gleams in the morning light. I climb aboard and the engine purrs to life. Cruising down Eleventh Street — the alias Route 66 uses as it snakes through Tulsa — I consider my good fortune. I am truly blessed to have the good sense to opt for a cruise down Route 66. Just my bike and miles of freedom. It's the perfect tonic.

Cyrus Avery Route 66 Memorial Bridge in Tulsa, before restoration

Only minutes out on the old road and already I'm feeling nothing but fine. I'm not worried about anything. On this weekend journey I have no reservations. Not a one. Don't need them. I'm on a scavenger hunt, an adventure. Time is meaningless.

I glide along beneath the shadows of art deco churches and palaces of commerce erected when Tulsa ruled as the "oil capitol of the world." Then I hook a left, cross the Arkansas River and ride westward. I have today's trek mapped out in my mind. I will hit a few "must see" sites including the Round Barn at Arcadia. But at the top of my list is a stop at one of my favorites — the Rock Cafe.

Round Barn, Arcadia

Between Tulsa and Oklahoma City, the Rock Cafe in the town of Stroud understands the value of comfort food. At least that's what I have found ever since I discovered the place years ago. I know the cafe has survived highway bypasses, oil busts, and killer tornadoes to emerge as one of the most resilient businesses on Route 66. Built of large sandstone rocks removed from the earth when highway workers carved the Route 66 roadbed, the cafe opened in 1939 and was an instant success. It soon became a bus stop for Greyhound. During World War II many young men took their sweethearts to the cafe before departing for military service and it was the first place they went when they came home.

I have encountered old-timers who consumed gallons of Rock Cafe coffee during ice storms. They sat there for days at a time watching trucks slide down the highway like hockey pucks. They spoke of power failures when cooks had to use the open fireplace to prepare meals and heat the place. Others remember pushing the jukebox to an open window so local kids could dance outside under the moonlight. I heard bitter memories as well — memories from the bad old days when black customers had to order their food at the back door and sit outside to eat.

The morning ride to Stroud is as good as any I've ever had. There are plenty of turns and curves along the two-lane highway and I realize that every time I venture out on Route 66 I find someone or something new. Each trip is different. I slow down for the small oil patch and farming towns and dodge ripe road kill. The Harley scoots over Little Polecat Creek and then Polecat Creek and passes tidy whitewashed homes with grand crops of roses, peonies, and irises the color of root beer and butterscotch.

Then Stroud appears and in a heartbeat the Rock Cafe comes into view. In decades past, the Rock's business plummeted for a while with the coming of the turnpike that left Stroud and so many other towns without much of a living. I know the Rock has gone through different owners, including a few who had no regard for the cafe's place on the historic highway or in the hearts of so many

people. But I also know that began to change in the early 1990s when a spunky young woman named Dawn Welch took over the Rock.

Satisfied bikers at the Rock Cafe, Stroud

As I begin to gear down and prepare to pull into the gravel parking lot, it's clear that business is not just good but booming. A fleet of motorcycles surrounds the entire cafe. Bikes are parked everywhere. Every make and model of Harley is present. It looks like a mini-Sturgis. I manage to slip my bike into a tight spot between two shiny Sportsters.

Bikers spill out the open front door and fill the patio. Many of them sit on their motorcycles gulping coffee and gobbling plates of breakfast. Inside it is pure mayhem. Every booth and table is filled with bikers and more of them stand along the walls. They are all laughing, talking, and either eating or trying to get served. By the time I arrive, a crew of the Rock's waitresses and cooks have reported for duty and are working alongside the bikers. Dawn's little daughter Alexis (a true child of

the Mother Road since her birthday falls on November 11, the date the highway become official in 1926) passes around a cafe guest ledger for the bikers to sign.

Enormous bikers covered in black leather and tattoos have donned aprons and help mix pancake batter and fry eggs in the kitchen while other bikers wash dishes, bus tables, and take food orders. Dawn and her husband Fred — big smiles on their faces — direct the action while a trio of attractive women bikers old enough to recall the sixties sing *Born to be Wild*.

A burly biker — shirtless in a leather vest — sits in a booth cradling Dawn and Fred's three-month-old son,

Bikers settle up bills at Rock Cafe, Stroud

Paul. The Harley rider coos at the baby snug in his tattooed arms and glares at anyone who gets too close. "I'm the designated baby sitter, " the big guy proudly tells me. I know without a doubt that this is the safest child in all of Oklahoma. So do little Paul's parents.

When all the eggs and milk are gone, several bikers race to a nearby convenience store to purchase fresh provisions with money from their own pockets. After more than an hour of table-hopping and making new friends, I manage to grab a chair and order some food. The buffalo burger I devour tastes like ambrosia and the bread pudding is so good one gnarly biker says he'd kill his mother for another bowl of the stuff.

Finally, as the crowd thins out and heads back to cruising the Mother Road, Dawn emerges from the kitchen and retrieves her baby. She pulls up a chair next to me and allows herself a few minutes of rest.

"It feels like we served just about every biker in the nation the last few days," she says. "Last night we stayed open until everyone was fed and then we crawled home

next door and collapsed. It was still dark this morning when they started arriving. We were in our pajamas and we opened up and started cooking. The bikers pitched right in and helped."

Dawn marvels that some of the bikers went to the market and bought their own food, cooked it, washed their dishes, and even paid for it again. They rotated in shifts as cooks and dishwashers but three women bikers stayed at the cash register throughout the entire episode making sure every check was covered and every bit of food and drink was paid for in full. Then a collection was taken up and Dawn and Fred were presented with a jar of money in honor of their new son.

With her baby boy tucked in her arms, Dawn returns to the kitchen to take stock and I drain my glass of ice water. Outside a pair of lovers sits side by side on their bikes beneath a big Chinese elm loaded with mistletoe. They kiss, ignite their engines, and then roar off down the road. I take my leave a few minutes later and never look back. I don't have to — I know I'll return. ∎

The Heart of the Mother Road

— ROBERT LOWERY

This story is in memory of Patricia McCabe Lowery.

I slowed my bike for the workers in reflective vests on the two-lane highway outside of Chandler, Oklahoma. We were on that stretch of Route 66 that carried so many Dust Bowlers, GI's, vacationers, and fellow bikers. The workers were replacing a section of the old road that had deteriorated beyond good sense, and the traffic narrowed to a single lane.

Sitting on the road in a jumble of gravel, concrete, and blacktop was a Bobcat with a drill attached to it. The drill pounded away at the blacktop and chips flew left and right. As I slowly passed the work-site, I noticed that the drill went all the way through the asphalt into the earth.

My wife, Pat, sitting in the passenger seat of our Harley-Davidson, nudged me from behind and said, "There's our piece of history."

I pulled ahead of the traffic until I found a safe siding off the road, where I parked the bike. I walked back to the foreman sitting in a pickup truck on the shoulder of the road. He was a friendly looking farm boy with lots of red hair, freckles, and a Caterpillar baseball cap perched on the back of his head.

"Can I help you?" he asked, in the accent of my grandfather and grandmother.

"How would you like to do an old man a big favor?" I said.

He guessed in a heartbeat what I was after. "You want a piece of old 66, don't you?"

"Yes, if it wouldn't be any trouble."

"None at all," he said, "there's more than enough to go around."

The foreman reached down to the floor on the passenger side of his truck and retrieved a paper bag. Then he removed the contents — a couple of sandwiches, a thermos, and a banana. He got out of the truck and as we walked toward the work site he handed me the bag. Neither of us spoke. He guessed that it was a solemn occasion.

The drilling had stopped and the machine sat idling. The drill had cut through a layer of blacktop, another of concrete, through gravel, and into the rich, red Oklahoma clay. The core of Route 66 was exposed.

Trembling, I reached under the dangling drill and scooped up three chunks. This was original 66 — Portland cement as tough as iron. I brushed off the sticky clay and gravel and carefully put the fragments into the sack. I nodded to the foreman, to the workers, to the Bobcat operator. The drill started again.

I turned and put the paper bag in my saddlebag. Then I got on my bike and we left. We were taking the remnants of history home. ■

Postscript from Robert: My wife, Pat, who accompanied me on all our Harley trips, died in February 2004. She was buried in a small churchyard cemetery in Wading River, New York. Mixed in with the soil that covers her coffin is a piece of Route 66.

"We found a rideable abandoned section of Route 66 before Erick, OK. It had to be a couple of miles long. Soon, others joined us, too. Each one of us felt like we had found a hidden treasure, a secret passageway...finding this "jewel" to ride. We were whooping and hollering the whole way! Fantastic!"

— Joy Schaub

Pop Hicks

—MICHAEL WALLIS

Pop Hicks Restaurant in Clinton, Oklahoma, was not only a Route 66 landmark but an American original. For generations of bikers, the historic restaurant was also a must stop — a place for down-home meals and, more importantly, friendly conversation. Since the doors first opened in 1936, Pop Hicks not only nourished bodies, it also nurtured souls.

For many of us it was a quintessential biker haven.

Howard and Mary Nichols, the last owners of this Mother Road institution — one of the oldest operating restaurants on Route 66 — helped create memories for travelers and local folks alike. They never met a stranger and road-weary bikers appreciated the warm reception and the chance to rest and refresh after a long spell in the saddle. At any given time there might be as many as a half-dozen bikes parked along the curb.

We stopped at Pop Hicks every time we traveled the Mother Road. We felt welcome day or night. Sometimes we encountered old gents and ladies sipping coffee at the liars' table, exhausted bikers gulping stout coffee, cheerleaders celebrating a football victory, or cowboys stoking up on breakfast. Thanks to the Nichols family and all the many good folks who worked there, we felt that we were at home at Pop Hicks. The people there were family. They always will be. We will never ever forget them and those special times on the open road.

On August 2, 1999, a fire erupted at Pop Hicks. Firemen raced to Clinton from several surrounding communities but flames consumed the building. It burned to the ground. There was no insurance and no way to rebuild. Now only a vacant space remains and motorists and bikers often slow down when they pass out of respect for the old times.

Rest in peace Pop Hicks. You served us well. ■

Two bikers with Howard Nicols at Pop Hicks

Recipes from Oklahoma

— MARIAN CLARK

At Waylan's Ku-Ku Burger in Miami, owner Gene Waylan says, "Don't just ask for a burger, ask for a Waylan's." This is one of the best hamburger stops in northeastern Oklahoma. The giant neon sign out front adds a nostalgic touch but the real quality here comes hot off the grill.

For those who enjoy an occasional break from hamburgers, try the chili dogs. Here is the giant recipe used to top the dogs.

Chili Dog Chili

WAYLAN'S KU-KU BURGER

7½ pounds chili meat, broken into small pieces
3 46-ounce cans tomato juice, with just enough
   water
to rinse cans
3 heaping tablespoons coarse grind pepper
3 heaping tablespoons salt
3 good handfuls of chopped onions
1 cup Williams Chili seasoning
1 #10 can of pinto beans, undrained

Combine all ingredients except chili seasoning and beans. Heat, stirring to prevent burning. Bring chili to a good boil then add the chili seasoning and cook mixture for 30 minutes. Puree beans in a blender or food processor and add to chili dog mixture. Stir well to blend. Freeze and store in several containers until needed.

FROM TROND MOBERG'S NOTES: "Laurel Kane knows how to make bikers feel welcome. On our last trip (September, 2003) she offered sandwiches for lunch. All of the sandwiches were marked with Norwegian names and there was no way we could pay her. I realize that this can't happen on a regular basis, but guess how much the road warriors appreciated this! The word-to-word effect of this is tremendous. Again, 66 is all about people."

Laurel Kane has quickly become the Route 66 ambassador in Afton. The former DX Station has come back to life under her careful guidance. A warm welcome awaits — this is a place to stop, stretch, learn about the surrounding area, and pick up some tempting snacks Laurel always has ready, like her famous beer cheese.

Afton Station Beer Cheese

2 cups shredded mild cheddar cheese
2 cups shredded sharp cheddar cheese
8 ounces beer (⅔ of a 12-ounce bottle)
3 cloves garlic
3 heaping tablespoons mayonnaise

Allow cheese to reach room temperature in a mixing bowl. (Meanwhile, drink the beer you're not planning to use.) Put garlic through a press and add to cheese. Place beer in saucepan and heat until just before the boiling point. Watch carefully so that it doesn't boil over. While beer is very hot, pour slowly over the cheese and garlic, stirring well. Add mayonnaise and continue to blend thoroughly. Mixture will be very soft.

Refrigerate for half an hour and stir again. Chill until ready to use.

Bring back to room temperature before serving. Good served with original flavor Bugles, pretzels, or rye bread sliced very thin. Approximately 3 cups.

Afton

VINITA IS THE UNCONTESTED "CALF FRY CAPITAL OF THE WORLD." The September festival each year provides an authentic glimpse of Oklahoma's Western heritage. There is plenty of good food and entertainment for everyone willing to try new experiences. This calf fry recipe comes from the Vinita Chamber of Commerce.

Oklahoma Calf Fries

Slice 2 pounds of Calf Fries about ¼ inch thick. (They are easier to slice if slightly frozen.)

Soak in an egg and milk mixture for about 10 minutes. Roll each fry in a mixture of 1½ cups cornmeal, 3 cups flour, and 1 teaspoon salt. Fry in hot oil (350 degrees) until golden brown. Enjoy.

Vinita

ALTHOUGH NEW TO THE ROAD, Vinita's Summerside Vineyards and Winery is already well known in Norway. In the summer of 2003, Trond Moberg reported that one of his road warriors had trouble with his bike and the whole caravan had to stop. It was 104 degrees when they pulled off the road near Vinita next to what looked like a construction site. "Out of the empty building came a lady who asked us all to come in since she had air conditioning. It turned out to be Marsha Butler, who was finishing the inside works at Summerside Vineyards and Winery. She said she would love to have us visit in 2004. She even offered box lunches and wine. Out of the blue we met another fine ambassador along 66. We will return!"

Summerside Route 66 Red Wine Drip Beef

1 three-pound boneless beef roast, trimmed
1 tablespoon garlic powder
½ teaspoon dried rosemary
3 cubes beef bouillon
1 cup Summerside Route 66 red wine
Water to cover

Combine beef with the garlic powder, rosemary, bouillon, wine and water. Simmer 8 or more hours in a Crock-pot until beef is tender. Remove meat and shred. Return to the au jus. Serve meat with barbecue sauce and hard rolls. 10-12 servings.

PHYLLIS DEWITT, A FORMER VINITA RESIDENT who now practices law in Tulsa, rides regularly with her biker husband, Tom. Besides their passion for motorcycles and the open road, they love barbecue. On weekends, Tom and Phyllis can often be found on their bike searching for new barbecue stops or revisiting old favorites. Phyllis has perfected this recipe for refried beans that incorporates great flavor and is low in fat.

Phyllis DeWitt's Refried Beans

1 pound dried pinto beans
1 boneless pork roast (1½ to 2 pounds)
1 tablespoon chili powder
2 teaspoons hot sauce
2 teaspoons cumin
3 cloves garlic, minced
1 tablespoon sugar
1½ to 2 teaspoons garlic salt
½ teaspoon salt

Wash beans thoroughly; cover with water and soak overnight. Drain beans and place in a large, heavy Dutch oven. Add pork roast and enough water to cover. Add remaining ingredients except garlic salt and salt.

Bring beans to boil and reduce heat to simmer, cooking 3½ to 4 hours. Remove the pork and shred. Mash the beans, add garlic salt and salt to taste.

Return ⅓ to ½ of the shredded pork to the beans, as desired. Serve beans with sour cream, guacamole, and/or cheese. 8 servings.

CABIN CREEK VINEYARD is another of northeast Oklahoma's newest tourism adventures.

With five acres of vineyards and a new tasting room, there is never a dull moment around here as family and friends plant, prune, pick and play under the Oklahoma sun. Rob and Pam Harris shared this great recipe that goes perfectly with the Rodeo Red wine they shared recently with a hefty group of Oklahoma City Harley-Davidson bikers who stopped at the winery during a recent cruise.

Hog Heaven Portabella App-a-teazers

Large firm portabella mushrooms rinsed well and
   dried
Cooking spray
Extra virgin olive oil
Garlic powder
Feta or Maytag Blue Cheese

Cabin Creek Vineyard Marinade:
¼ cup Rodeo Red Cabernet
2 tablespoons butter, melted
1 teaspoon hot raspberry Thunder Sauce
Touch of honey
Dash of Greek seasoning
Fresh black pepper

Topping:
Feta or Maytag blue cheese

Spray grill with cooking spray and set to low/medium heat. Coat mushrooms with olive oil and dust with garlic powder. Combine all marinade ingredients and brush mushrooms with marinade. Place mushrooms on grill and continue to brush with marinade while mushrooms are cooking, about 10 minutes depending on size. Top with Feta or Maytag Blue Cheese. Serve with Cabin Creek Vineyard Rodeo Red wine and enjoy.

CLAREMORE IS HOME TO THE HAMMETT HOUSE, one of the best-known eating places in northeastern Oklahoma. Owners, Bill and Linda Biard, take pride in their special "pamper" fried chicken, potato rolls, and fourteen varieties of humongous pies. Bikers never go away hungry here.

Lemon Pecan Pie
HAMMETT HOUSE

6 whole eggs
⅓ stick margarine, melted
2¼ cups sugar
¾ cup pecan pieces
1 teaspoon lemon extract
Juice of ½ a lemon
8-inch unbaked pie shell

Mix ingredients in order given, but do not use a mixer or beat until frothy. Pour into pie shell. Place in preheated 350 degree oven and bake 10 minutes. Reduce oven temperature to 300 degrees and bake until crust is browned and pie is set. 6 slices.

AT CATOOSA'S ANNUAL LIBERTYFEST CELEBRATION, three days of outdoor fun surround the Fourth of July holiday. The most popular activity is the Chili Cook-off. Joe Giles, a recent winner, is an avid chili cook who has won first place in the Arkansas, Oklahoma, Missouri, and Kansas Mens' State Championships and has produced a winning bowl of fire at the annual Terlingua Cook-off. Joe promises that diced raw apple alongside every steaming bowl of his chili makes a perfect accompaniment. I followed his advice and agree!

Loose Stool Chili
Libertyfest July Fourth Celebration — 1995
First Prizewinning Recipe
PERPETRATED BY JOE GILES

2 pounds of cubed lean stew meat
Enough water to cover
1 eight-ounce can tomato sauce
1 tablespoon Le Gout beef base
2 teaspoons onion powder
1½ teaspoon garlic powder
½ teaspoon garlic salt
1 teaspoon white pepper
1 teaspoon MSG
5½ teaspoons chili powder
1 tablespoon cumin
⅛ teaspoon cayenne
Salt and pepper to taste

Cover the stew meat with water and boil for 45 minutes.

Add tomato sauce, beef base, and the "white spices" of onion powder, garlic powder, garlic salt, pepper and MSG. Boil for 25 minutes, stirring occasionally. Add "red spices" of chili powder, cumin, and cayenne. Simmer for 35 minutes, stirring frequently. Add salt and pepper to taste just before serving. 6-8 servings.

Catoosa

Honky Tonkin'

Go honky tonkin' in these Tulsa country and western dance clubs:
Redneck Kountry, 19011 E. Admiral Blvd.
Caravan Cattle Company, 7901 41st St.
Midnight Rodeo, 9379 E. 46th St.
Cain's Ballroom, 423 N. Main

PROOF THAT OKLAHOMA IS A BIKER PARADISE comes with two thriving Harley-Davidson dealerships in Tulsa. Larry and Pat Wofford own a twenty-year-old family business they purchased in December of 1998. They quickly changed the name and became the first Harley-Davidson dealer in the nation to combine the two famous icons — Route 66 and Harley-Davidson.

Attaching himself to the mystique of the road was one of Wofford's many wise moves.

"Route 66 is basically every two-laner out there," says Wofford. "The difference between it and a modern freeway is like being in a car or being on a Harley; it's two different ways of viewing the world." Their new 32,500-square-feet facility, dedicated to both images, easily earned the *Dealernews Magazine* "Best Use of a Theme" honors in 2003. *Dealership* covers the entire "power-sport" industry.

You can find Larry and Pat and their enthusiastic staff at Route 66 Harley-Davidson, 3637 South Memorial. Route 66 has truly paved their way to success. Pat shared this menu that is sure to please folks at every Harley get-together.

TAKE ME BACK TO TULSA TENDERLOIN

CHICAGO BLUE CHEESE POTATOES

BARSTOW BEER BATTERED ONION RINGS

ST. LOUIS SPINACH SALAD DEATH VALLEY DEVILED EGGS

BRISTOW BLONDE BOMBSHELL BROWNIES

Take Me Back to Tulsa Tenderloin

1 (3-pound) pork loin

Marinade:
½ cup Jack Daniels whiskey
½ cup balsamic vinegar
1 cup orange juice, divided
1 tablespoon garlic powder

Combine whiskey, vinegar, ½ cup of the orange juice, and garlic powder. Blend well. Place tenderloin in a large freezer-weight sealable plastic bag. Pour marinade over meat. Seal bag and refrigerate overnight. Remove meat and discard the marinade.

Bake tenderloin in a preheated 350 degree oven for 1½ hours. Pour remaining ½ cup orange juice over meat. Insert a meat thermometer into the thickest part. Bake an additional 10 to 30 minutes or until internal temperature reaches 160 degrees. Let meat stand 10 minutes before slicing to serve. Serve with juices from pan. 8 servings.

Chicago Blue Cheese Potatoes

3 medium-sized baking potatoes, unpeeled and
    thinly sliced
1½ cups whipping cream
2 tablespoons butter, melted
1 tablespoon minced garlic
1 teaspoon salt
½ teaspoon white pepper
½ cup (2 ounces) crumbled blue cheese

Place potatoes in a greased 10x6x2-inch baking dish. Combine next 5 ingredients and pour over potatoes. Bake, uncovered, in a preheated 400 degree oven for 40 minutes. Sprinkle with cheese and bake an additional 5 minutes. 4-6 servings.

Western Oklahoma

The Great American Bunion Derby

Promoted as "C.C. Pyle's First Annual International Trans-Continental Footrace," the 1928 Bunion Derby promoted a marathon run from Los Angeles to New York City.

Andy Payne, a young, un-employed, part-Cherokee from the Route 66 town of Foyil, Oklahoma, won the race and the impressive prize of $25,000. With the money, Andy paid off his parent's farm and married his sweetheart.

The footrace attracted runners from around the world. Over 200 entrants, ranging in age from 16 to 64, left the Los Angeles Speedway on March 4, 1928. Fifty-five men finished the race with Andy outdistancing them all. He arrived in New York City after 84 days, having run 3423.3 miles. His winning time was 573 hours and 4 minutes.

C.C. Pyle, who had hoped to get rich and make a name for himself with the event, barely made expenses and was never able to mount another race.

Besides Andy's success, the other major winner of the Bunion Derby was the National US Highway 66 Association. The marathon brought national attention to the highway and was the first event to place Highway 66 in the forefront of road recognition.

FROM *PRETTY BOY: THE LIFE AND TIMES OF CHARLES ARTHUR FLOYD,* BY MICHAEL WALLIS:

When Pretty Boy was not on the outlaw trail making "withdrawals" from banks, he loved to get into the kitchen and bake apple pie. In 1933 one of his pies won top honors at a country pie supper where the respected sheriff, unaware of who had done the baking, tasted the slice and declared it the best pie he'd ever put in his mouth.

The thirty-year-old bandit left an apple pie behind in his Buffalo, New York hideaway when, in 1934, he decided to head toward home in Sallisaw. On that trip, a final shootout ended his life, and he never saw Oklahoma again.

This pie recipe is considered Pretty Boy's best version:

Michael Wallis's Pretty Boy's Apple Pie

Pie Crust:
2 cups flour
¾ cup lard
1 teaspoon salt
6-7 tablespoons cold water

Prepare crust by working the flour, lard, and salt together until crumbly. Mix in cold water until dough holds together in big pieces. Divide into two equal balls.

On a floured surface roll out one ball thin enough to line a 9-inch pie tin. Roll out second ball for the top crust.

Preheat oven to 450 degrees.

Apple Filling:
1 pound fresh apples, peeled and sliced or
    1 (16-ounce) can
2 tablespoons fresh lemon juice
½ teaspoon ground nutmeg
½ teaspoon ground cinnamon
½ cup white sugar
¼ cup seedless raisins
1 cup brown sugar
2 tablespoons flour
2 tablespoons butter
½ cup shelled Oklahoma pecans
¼ cup milk

Hard Sauce:
½ cup butter
1½ cups powdered sugar
1 tablespoon boiling water
1 tablespoon brandy or rum (moonshine is preferable)

Place the apples in the lined pan. Sprinkle with lemon juice, nutmeg, and cinnamon. Spread the white sugar and raisins evenly over the apples. Mix the brown sugar, flour and butter in a bowl. When well blended, spread over the apples and sprinkle with pecans. Add most of the milk and cover with the top crust. Seal the edges and prick top with a fork. Brush the remaining milk on the crust.

Bake for 10 minutes at 450 degrees, then reduce heat to 350 degrees and bake another 30 minutes until crust is golden.

To make hard sauce, cream the butter until light. Beat in the sugar, add water, and then beat in the liquor. Serve sauce on each slice of pie. If you dare, add a scoop of homemade vanilla ice cream.

REBA MCCLANAHAN IS THE BUSY HANDS-ON OWNER of Myers-Duren Harley-Davidson in Tulsa. The business is Oklahoma's oldest Harley dealership and possibly the third oldest in the nation.

In addition, Reba is one of the very few women owners of a Harley franchise nationwide.

McClanahan is only the third owner of this Tulsa dealership that opened in 1912 and once thrived on Route 66. Today, she operates her flourishing dealership from a custom-designed art deco showplace at 4848 South Peoria Avenue.

By all counts, Reba McClanahan is an outstanding cook. She regularly serves a holiday buffet for Harley-Davidson friends at her South Peoria location in Tulsa and shared these favorites from past celebrations. Her favorite barbecued meatball recipe is mutually shared by Debbie Pruitt in the *Sapulpa Daily Herald* and follows these recipes.

Reba McClanahan's Sausage Balls

2 cups biscuit mix (Bisquick)
2 cups grated Cheddar cheese
1 pound hot sausage
3 tablespoons water

Mix all ingredients together and roll into small balls. Bake in a preheated 350 degree oven for 15-20 minutes. About 100 1-inch balls

Reba McClanahan's Beef Boat Dip

3 jars (2.25 ounce each) dried beef, minced
1⅓ cups low-fat mayonnaise
1⅓ cups sour cream
2 tablespoons minced onion
2 tablespoons chopped parsley
2 teaspoons dill weed
2 teaspoons Beau Monde
Chopped green onion to taste
1 loaf round pumpernickel bread, unsliced

Combine all ingredients except the bread. Mix well and let stand overnight in the refrigerator.

Hollow out the loaf of bread and fill with beef mixture. Serve with crackers.

EACH NOVEMBER, the *Sapulpa Daily Herald* holds a recipe contest and publishes a cookbook under the direction of Laurie Quinnelly, Lifestyle Editor. A panel of eight judges recently gave these two recipes the winning nod. They are both comfort dishes of the highest order!

Sapulpa

Debbie Pruitt's Barbecued Meatballs

3 pounds lean ground beef
1 12-ounce can evaporated milk
1 cup oatmeal
1 cup cracker crumbs
2 eggs
½ cup finely chopped onion
½ teaspoon garlic powder
2 teaspoons salt
½ teaspoon pepper
2 teaspoons chili powder

Combine all ingredients. Mixture will be soft. Shape into walnut-size balls. Place meatballs in a single layer on a waxed-paper lined cookie sheet. Freeze until firm. Store meatballs in freezer bag until ready to use.

Sauce for meatballs:
2 cups catsup
1 cup brown sugar
½ teaspoon liquid smoke
½ teaspoon garlic powder
¼ cup finely chopped onion

Combine all ingredients and stir until sugar is dissolved. Place frozen meatballs in 9x13-inch baking pan. Pour sauce over meat. Bake in preheated 350 degree oven for one hour. Serve while warm, preferably in chafing dish. 60-70 walnut-sized meatballs.

Jeanie Thoos Spradlin's Holiday Bread Pudding with Whiskey Sauce

1 10-ounce loaf French bread, 2-3 days old
(or 6-8 cups dry, crumbled bread)
4 cups milk
2 cups sugar
½ cup butter, melted
3 eggs
2 tablespoons vanilla
1 cup raisins
1 cup coconut
1 cup shopped pecans
1 teaspoon cinnamon
1 teaspoon nutmeg

Combine all ingredients to form a moist mixture. Pour into a buttered 9x12 baking dish. Place in a non-preheated oven and bake for 1 hour and 15 minutes at 350 degrees, or until pudding is golden brown. Serve warm with whiskey sauce.

Whiskey Sauce:

½ cup butter

1½ cups powdered sugar

2 egg yolks

½ cup bourbon, scotch, rum or fruit juice

Cream butter and sugar over medium heat until butter melts and sugar is dissolved. Remove from heat and add egg yolk. Pour liquor into mixture gradually, stirring constantly. Sauce will thicken as it cools. Serve warm over the bread pudding. 10-12 servings.

Locals call the stretch of Route 66 between Tulsa and Oklahoma City the "free road." In 1953 when the Turner Turnpike became the first interstate to transplant Route 66, the turnpike became a toll road. To this day many locals continue to avoid the turnpike, taking the free road instead. It is a superb biker route.

BRISTOW WAS ORIGINALLY SETTLED by Lebanese immigrants whose descendants share the foods we all have grown to love. Lebanese cooks impart a special touch to tabouleh, even though the dish appears in the cuisine of many other Middle Eastern cultures.

Tabouleh

8 ounces bulgur (fine cracked wheat)

5 bunches parsley, stems removed and finely chopped

1 pound ripe tomatoes, finely chopped

5 green onions, finely chopped

2 tablespoons fresh mint leaves, minced

⅛ teaspoon allspice (optional)

½ cup lemon juice (adjust to taste)

½ cup olive oil

Salt and pepper to taste

Cover the bulgur in cold water and soak for 1 hour. Squeeze dry. Pick the parsley leaves from the large stems. Discard stems. Wash and dry parsley leaves. Chop all vegetables. Mix parsley, tomatoes, onions, and mint together. Combine allspice, lemon juice and olive oil. Pour over bulger and toss lightly. Salt and pepper to taste. 20 small servings.

THE ROCK CAFE, now on the National Register of Historic Places, has experienced a renaissance under the capable guidance of Dawn Welch. This 1939 vintage eatery celebrated 66 years on Route 66 in 2005. It remains a second home to thousands of cross-country truckers, bikers, and 66 enthusiasts as well as a favorite hangout for locals. The giraffe stone exterior came from the roadbed when Route 66 was built through the area. A recent grant has helped Dawn refurbish the interior and a warm welcome can be found just inside the doors. Bikers are always welcome and find this to be a memorable stop.

Dawn shared this recipe for her success: "Ingredients: Combine equal amounts of nostalgia, kindness, and a sense of family. Add this to the cook's good attitude and waitresses who are always ready to talk. And never, never forget to add love to taste."

Rock Cafe Old Fashioned Greasy Hamburger

¼ pound coarsely ground beef
½ teaspoon salt, or to taste
¼ teaspoon pepper
1 teaspoon finely chopped onion

Mix all ingredients, lightly pat into a burger about ½ inch thick. For a juicy burger, don't pack the meat. If the meat is too lean, mix a little ground suet with the patty. Fry patty on grill or in iron skillet for a few minutes, turn and cook a few minutes longer. Overcooking dries out the meat.

Lightly butter the top and bottom of a bun, place on grill until golden brown. Spread mustard on bottom half, pile with chopped onions, pickles, and meat patty. Spread mayonnaise or mustard on top half of bun. Pat the top of the bun with a spatula loaded with hamburger grease. Add lettuce, tomato, and catsup as desired. 1 old-fashioned burger.

BRUSH THE DUST OFF YOUR LEATHERS and stop for a spell at Hillbillee's Cafe in Arcadia. This is a place made for bikers! Wade and Norma Braxton will make you feel right at home. There's live music several nights each week and a top-notch place to stay nearby in their remodeled log cabin bed and breakfast.

City Slicker Chicken
HILLBILLEE'S CAFE

Grill an unbreaded, unskinned chicken breast in 1 tablespoon olive oil for about 4-5 minutes. Season with a touch of basil, salt, and freshly ground black pepper. Finely chop 2 green onions, 1 slice of bell pepper and a small piece of fresh ginger root. Sprinkle on grill to gently sear. Place on top of grilled chicken breast. Serve with slices of tomato and potato salad. 1 serving.

CHERYL NOWKA LIVES IN LAS VEGAS TODAY, but grew up on Route 66 in Hydro, Oklahoma. Her mom, Lucille Hamons, passed away in August of 2000 and loved her title of "The Mother of the Mother Road." The spirit of Lucille Hamons still reigns at her old home and gas station on Route 66 near Hydro. Nostalgia-loving friends continue to erect memorials almost daily, leaving notes, flowers, crosses, and totems, taking away their very own camera images filled with a bit of highway magic. Lucille's is the atypical site: once a grocery store / carryout / gas station / beer source / tourist court / shrine, and home to countless thousands, it still welcomes highway travelers on the undulating strip of 66 within a stones throw of I-40. When I visited with her just a few weeks before her death in 2000, Lucille had her memory book of famous autographs on the table beside her chair and told me again that memories kept her going. Age, moisture, and termites have settled in at the old structure where many a story has unfolded behind the prolific ivy covering. Folks from the Smithsonian have moved her Hamons Court sign to Washington.

Cheryl shared this favorite margarita recipe and reminded me, "Mom was very partial to her biker visitors. I hope she, Kirk Woodward, and Cheryl Cory are sitting around talking 66 as we speak."

Cheryl's Margaritas

1 cup of ice cubes placed in blender
4 ounces Jose Cuervo Gold tequila poured over the ice
4 ounces of Triple Sec poured over ice and tequila
6 ounce can frozen Minute Maid limeade
1 cup water

Always place ice cubes in blender first. Add remaining ingredients. Blend until smooth.

Don't pour yet! Halve and quarter a lime, rub the flesh of the lime around edge of glass rims 2-3 times and immediately dip in fine popcorn salt. Pour those margaritas and enjoy.

KAMP'S GROCERY AT 1310 CLASSEN, OKLAHOMA CITY, is a hidden treasure amidst the bustle of state capital traffic. Locals flock to Kamp's for the deli menu and great box lunches, as well as the family dinners to go, all in conjunction with the *Yippee-Yi-Yo Cafe* inside the 1910-vintage store.

The place remains a mecca from the past — tin ceilings, wood floors, old fixtures, and plenty of photographs. The croissant sandwich is typical of the good food served at the deli.

88

Kamp's Grocery Smoked Turkey Croissant

1 fresh croissant
4 ounces thinly sliced smoked turkey breast
1 teaspoon tarragon mayonnaise
Lettuce
Tomato slices
1 tablespoon Gorgonzola Vinaigrette

Toast the croissant. Heat the turkey. Place turkey, mayonnaise, lettuce and tomato on half the croissant. Top with Gorgonzola vinaigrette. 1 sandwich.

Gorgonzola Vinaigrette:
4 ounces Gorgonzola cheese
4 ounces olive oil
2 ounces balsamic vinegar

Combine and stir until well blended. Will keep in refrigerator for 2 weeks when well sealed. Use as needed for salads and sandwiches.

WOMEN WHO HAVE SPENT A LONG DAY IN THE SADDLE appreciate an easy meal. Here is a perfect suggestion shared by Johnita and Lionel Turner from the Willow Way Bed and Breakfast near Oklahoma City's Remington Park.

Aunt Kay's Brisket

5-7 pound trimmed brisket
(10-12 pounds untrimmed)

Sprinkle generously with the following:

Garlic salt
Onion salt
Lowery's seasoned salt
Meat tenderizer

Place meat in a large cooking bag and add a mixture of:

4 tablespoons liquid smoke
4 tablespoons Worcestershire
3 tablespoons soy sauce
3 tablespoons Italian dressing
2 tablespoons catsup
1 teaspoon prepared mustard
1 teaspoon celery seed

Marinate overnight. Bake in cooking bag in a preheated 275 degree oven for 4-5 hours or until tender. Begin testing at about 3½ hours in order not to overcook meat. Slice after meat has cooled and serve with basting juice. 12 or more servings.

CALUMET IS A QUIET COMMUNITY, a place where pioneer family members are close-knit and comfortable. Pat Lafoe of Calumet shared this all-time favorite cookie recipe originally prepared by her mother. These cookies fit perfectly in a tank bag.

Pat Lafoe's Oatmeal Cookies

1 cup margarine
1 cup brown sugar
1 cup granulated sugar
1 teaspoon vanilla
2 eggs, well beaten
1½ cups flour
3 cups oatmeal
1 teaspoon soda
1 teaspoon salt
1 teaspoon cinnamon
½ cup raisins (optional)

Cream margarine and add sugar, vanilla, and eggs. Add dry ingredients and mix well. Drop by teaspoonful on ungreased cookie sheet. Bake in preheated 350 degree oven for 10 minutes.
100 cookies.

TIRES SING ON THE OLD CONCRETE in this area and weeds continue to encroach. It's a section of real history waiting to be ridden. In Elk City, a 1920 prairie home has been transformed into the Country Dove where arguably, the best French silk pie on Route 66 is served. Glenna Hollis and Kay Farmer will make you feel right at home. Even rough-and-tumble bikers are welcome.

French Silk Pie
COUNTRY DOVE

Nut Crust:
1 stick butter, melted
1 cup flour
⅔ cup finely chopped nuts

Filling:
¾ cup butter
1⅓ cups sugar
2 teaspoons vanilla
2 squares unsweetened chocolate, melted and cooled
3 large eggs

Whipped Cream Topping:
½ pint whipping cream
¼ cup sugar
1 teaspoon vanilla
Chocolate shavings

Combine crust ingredients and blend well. Pat a thin layer of mixture into bottom and sides of a 10-inch pie pan. Bake in preheated 350 degree oven for 20 minutes. Allow to cool.

Cream butter and sugar thoroughly. Blend in vanilla and chocolate and mix well. Add eggs one at a time, beating with mixer on high speed for at least 5 minutes after each addition. Pour mixture into pie shell and chill in refrigerator for several hours or overnight. The crust and filling freeze well at this stage if making the pie ahead of time.

Whip cream to soft peak stage. Add sugar and vanilla and continue to whip until cream stands in firm peaks. Spread over pie and grate sweetened chocolate on top. 8 slices.

OKRA AND BLACK-EYED PEAS are almost always found in Oklahoma gardens. Kay Atkins shared her mother, Rosalee Admire's, favorite okra salad. Rosalee was a child of ten in 1928 when the Bunion Derby took place. She remembers being very scared of the strangers as they came running by her home. The men were all thirsty, so she overcame her fear and was soon providing water as they paused briefly on their run down Route 66.

Rosalee Admire's Fried Okra Salad

6 slices bacon, fried crisp and drained
2 tomatoes, chopped
1 small onion, chopped
½ bell pepper, chopped
1 large bag (20 ounce) frozen okra, or 4 cups home
    grown okra,
fried, drained, and cooled

Dressing:
⅓ cup vinegar
¼ cup sugar
¼ cup vegetable oil

Fry the bacon and set aside. Combine the tomatoes, onion, pepper, and okra. Mix the vinegar, sugar, and vegetable oil in a jar and shake until blended. Crumble the bacon over the vegetables and pour the dressing over all just before serving. 8 servings.

Note: This salad is good even without the dressing!

ON THE HIGHWAY 66 CURVE heading west from Texola, the Last Stop Bar has a freshly sign painted on its front wall:

"There's no other place
Like this place
Anywhere near this place
So this must be the place." ■

The Highway's Heyday

— MICHAEL WALLIS

During World War II, a shotage of gasoline and tires meant civilians could only dream about road trips on America's Main Street, a highway filled instead with troop convoys and GI's hitchhiking home. But the years following the war proved to be the heyday of motor travel, especially on Route 66.

I was born in St. Louis in 1945, just as the troops marched home to start new jobs, build homes, and take vacations in big gas-guzzling cars. By 1950, my family was in the midst of the pack cruising Route 66, taking in all the natural and manmade attractions. I saw my first real cowboys and Indians, spied my first oil well, and ate my first enchilada platter on the Mother Road.

Just the act of "getting there" was an important part of our travel experience. When the tires of our family sedan hit the pavement, it was official — the vacation had begun. Every single moment counted. Windows were cranked down as Dad mashed the gas pedal to the floor. The radio purred and I dreamed of outlaw hideouts, snake farms, cheeseburgers and thick chocolate malts. The potential for high adventure lurked around every curve. The fantasy had begun. ∎

Texas

Fast facts from Texas

- Cross the panhandle in 177 miles on Route 66.

- Chili is the official state dish and the jalapeño is the official state pepper. Grapefruit is the official fruit. The state animal is the armadillo.

- Palo Duro Canyon State Park, south of Amarillo, is the second largest canyon in the United States, covering 15,103 acres.

- Two official state rest stops near McLean are now the most elaborate along all of Route 66 (I-40), they even include tornado shelters. One is themed Route 66, the other pays tribute to the pioneer farming and ranching history of the area.

Texas Biker Road Rules

- Safety Helmet, required until rider passes test and shows proof of $10,000 hospitalization insurance

- Eye Protection, not required

Must see in Texas

- SHAMROCK
  - The tallest water tower in Texas
  - U Drop Inn — Resplendent with new paint and new neon, the art deco architecture now houses city offices and a visitors' center.

U Drop Inn, Shamrock

- MCLEAN
  - Devil's Rope and Old Route 66 Museum, corner of Kingsley and Old Route 66. This jewel of a museum is one of the best along Route 66, not to be missed.

Devil's Rope and Old Route 66 Museum, McLean

- Restored 1930s Phillips 66 station on old westbound Route 66

- GROOM — "Cross of the Lord Jesus Christ" looms 190 feet tall and contains 75 tons of steel. It is the tallest cross in the western hemisphere. Note: This has been the scene of numerous biker and trucker weddings.

Restored 1930s Phillips 66 station, McLean

The Lone Star State

Amarillo
● 66

Dallas
●

TEXAS

●**El Paso**

Austin ★

Houston
●

●
San Antonio

- The Britten USA Tower built intentionally with one short leg

- *AMARILLO* — Take a 30 minute detour to Palo Duro Canyon State Park stretching 110 majestic miles south of Amarillo. See *"Texas"* the outstanding summer musical drama in the dramatic outdoor theater in Palo Duro Canyon.

- Find "Art for Art's Sake" traffic signs. Stanley Marsh 3 has the city talking again. Over 750 signs have gone up (and come down) sporting a wide range of unusual statements.

The Britten USA Tower

- Cadillac Ranch, west edge of Amarillo on I-40 and Route 66. Ten vintage Cadillac models planted in a row with tail fins pointing skyward at the same angle as the Cheops' pyramids. Stanley Marsh 3's favorite art

- *VEGA* — Authentic Texas cattle country, the area was once a part of the famous XIT Ranch, land of the Llano Estacado, America's staked plains. Terrain is pancake flat along here and the wind always blows. (Inexperienced bikers take heed.)

- Adrian — Midpoint along Route 66.

- Glenrio — Ghost town where the decaying corpse of "First in Texas, Last in Texas" Motel and Cafe sign presides over the empty street by the wooden state line marker. Put one foot in Deaf Smith County, Texas, the other in Quay County, New Mexico.

Beacon in the dark

- Big Texan Motel, 7701 I-40 East

Stanley Marsh 3's Cadillac Ranch — Kazyo Omiya from Japan, "Cruisin'" Susan Daly, Helen Horn, Kyoko Omiya (Japan), "Milwaukee" Harry Jaeger

Favorite hangouts for food and drink

- MCLEAN — Red River Steak House. On Friday and Saturday nights Tye Thompson's mesquite smoke-flavored mouth-watering barbecue and prime rib are served. Tye is the artist who has done numerous 66 murals on area buildings.

- GROOM — Route 66 Steakhouse, formerly the Golden Spread Grill, Old Highway 66. A recommended biker-friendly stop for steaks

- AMARILLO —
  - Indulge in a Cowboy Morning Breakfast

Route 66 Steakhouse, Groom

or Cowboy Evening Dinner on the rim of Palo Duro Canyon.
  - Big Texan Steak Ranch, 7701 I-40 East. Home to the 72-ounce steak, Big Texan Opry Stage, Saturday morning cowboy poetry, and Reptile Ranch, which houses one of the largest western diamondback rattlesnakes in Texas
  - The Golden Light, 2908 West 6th. The oldest cafe that has remained in the same location in Amarillo — great hamburgers
  - Blue Front Cafe, 801 West 6th. Comfortable and friendly. The stop where you can try Amarillo's version of the famous pig hip sauce!
  - Beans and Things, 700 Amarillo Blvd. East (Old 66). Some of the finest barbecue and chili you will find in Texas. Look for the cow on top! Highly recommended

- ADRIAN — Mid-Point Cafe. A not-to-be-missed location

Father's Day

— BOB "CROCODILE" LILE

I've been riding cycles forever and have been just about everywhere my bike can take me, but my jaunts up and down Route 66 rank among my best ever. One in particular stands out in my mind. It wasn't even very long — only a few days on the Mother Road in Texas and New Mexico — but that ride has never left me.

My son Chris came along. I was excited since it was to be our first trip together on motorcycles. Although I was a bit fretful about his riding my Heritage Softail, I looked forward to the two of us being together out on the open road. He was twenty-six and I was fifty-eight and we had not had any real one-on-one time since his mother and I split up in 1986. Now we had this gift of time to share.

Chris lived in Amarillo. He rode out and spent the night before our departure at my place in the country. We got up early the next morning, drank a pot of coffee, and hit the road, hoping to miss the afternoon rains that visit the Texas Panhandle in September. Just in case, as we rode back toward Amarillo, we decided to swing by Chris's house to pick up his rain gear.

We cruised westward and I thought about my boy and how he had grown up. I used to get so disappointed when he was a little guy and would always want to go play and not tend to his obligations. He was a sweet kid though — curly hair, big flashing eyes, and that grin that could make friends with nearly everyone. I was proud of the way he got along with others. I knew that he was drawn to the underdogs who didn't stand a chance

instead of taking up with the smarter and richer kids. I admired him for that even though it got him into trouble more than once.

Still, I guessed I was lucky. I had raised four sons and not one of them had ever been in any real serious trouble. Chris was the only one of the bunch to even spend a night in jail. Happened when he was eighteen and he got picked up for outstanding traffic warrants. He was too broke to take care of the fines. I'll never forget that phone call. I told him that if he was gonna dance then he had to pay the band. I also told him to get a job, join the Marines, or go to school.

"I'll help you anyway you pick to go," I said, " but I will not help you become a bum."

All sorts of thoughts and memories ran through my mind as my bike raced on and those shiny chromed wheels sliced through the wind. There is nothing quite like it. One side of your mind is free to wander and the other side takes care of the business at hand on the road.

We approached Amarillo and as we did we passed by the Clements Unit and the Neal Unit correctional facilities. We used to call these places prisons but now that won't do and we call them units. Sounds like we're talking about college dorms. Anyway as we passed the prisons, out of the corner of my eye I spied a group of inmates working along a barbed wire fence on the perimeter. There were ten or twelve of them and three guards. One guard was on horseback and all three of them had rifles and wore those mirrored sunglasses.

I glanced over and just as we got even with them, all the prisoners stopped working, stood at attention, and raised their right arms in a closed-fisted salute. It took a few seconds to register and then chills ran down my spine. Just the sound of those two Harleys running down the road was the ultimate sound of freedom. I glanced back and saw that the guards were stunned. My mind raced. Thank God, none of my boys are in there, I thought.

We made the run into Amarillo, side by side, my brain in overdrive. When we pulled in at Chris's place, he got off his bike and said, "Dad, did you see that? Did you see those men salute us?" He was as amazed as I was that a couple of guys on motorcycles could have that kind of impact.

For the next few days I thought about those inmates and I wondered what they dreamed about that night. I bet they dreamed they were riding bikes down a two-lane going anywhere they wanted to go. My heart ached because I knew that not all of them belonged there.

Chris and I didn't talk about it after that. We just enjoyed being together on the old road in New Mexico. We rode the mountains, the desert, and dipped into Billy the Kid country. It was pure quality time.

Now years later the image of those prisoners haunts me. I never ride that way without thinking about that morning and those men in silent unison saluting what we take for granted — a motorcycle, an open road to freedom, and time spent with someone you love. It still makes me cry. ■

The Big Texan

— MICHAEL WALLIS

The Big Texan Steak Ranch — a Route 66 favorite for years — moved to the super slab in 1970 when Interstate 40 muscled its way past the Amarillo city limits, and the restaurant's business plummeted overnight. Today, however, this Panhandle landmark has evolved into a Route 66 veteran that thumbs its nose at the generic cookie-cutter joints crowding the interstate highway. That is why friends of the Mother Road still stop to tangle with grilled beef served in all manners and sizes.

The Big Texan Steak Ranch, Amarillo

True to the old road adage that every business has to have a gimmick to draw folks inside, the Big Texan has become legendary because of its widely advertised promise of free 72-ounce steaks to all-comers. Of course there is a catch. Besides having to devour all of the four-and-a-half-pounds of beef in order to get the meal at no charge, diners must also consume a baked potato, shrimp cock-tail, dinner salad, and a buttered roll. Oh, and by the way, they have to clean their plate in one hour or less. If they cannot eat everything, then they fork over fifty bucks.

Most of the thousands who try this gastronomical feat fail to beat the clock. Only a select few succeed and see their name and time posted on the winner's board. Through the years I have witnessed all sorts of people boldly march into the Big Texan and attempt to get the best of the slab of beef the size of a doormat.

Wisely, I have never taken any dares and tried to eat the monster steak myself. I would much rather watch the blue-haired ladies, little boys, truckers, cowboys, German tourists, and about every facet of humanity you can imagine sit down and give it a go. I knew an old bowlegged fellow from Shamrock who ate the big steak four times a year and each and every time he did it he first removed his dentures before he started eating.

Harley celebration on 6th Street, Amarillo

Still my favorite giant steak challengers to watch at the Big Texan have always been the bikers. They put on the best show of all.

Corey Hebert (right) winning Big Texan challenge, Amarillo

How can I forget observing an array of Harley riders, including a couple of pretty gnarly fellows, engage in a Big-Texan-sponsored steak-eating contest during a shindig on Sixth Street, the old Mother Road route through Amarillo? It was quite a scene and the winner — Corey Hebert, a young man from Milwaukee — not only bested all the others but also, true to his word, did somersaults down the Mother Road as soon as he was declared the steak-eating champ.

But my best recollection of the Big Texan is when two broad-shouldered bikers dueled it out before a huge crowd gathered at the restaurant. Both contenders appeared confident and ready. They sat side by side in chairs fashioned from steer horns at an elevated table with a big digital clock ready to start ticking. The rules of the contest were solemnly read out loud and — with bibs in place and knives and forks in their mitts — the pair mugged for their cheering biker well wishers. The signal was given and the battle commenced.

Almost immediately I spotted the biker who I felt would ultimately win. He made all the right moves of a steak eating pro, such as quickly drinking down the shrimp cocktail as if it were a shot of tequila. With that out of the way, he steadily alternated bites of the spud and salad with the enormous steak and he took only small sips from his glass of ice tea. Smart guy.

Meanwhile his opponent turned all his attention to the steak and neglected the side dishes. He also slugged down big gulps of his beverage. In no time at all he was bloated. Clearly this man was doomed to flounder and fail.

About twenty minutes into the contest, the more skillful biker started looking at the other man's plate. Then he leaned over and quietly asked if he could have some of his opponent's steak since his was almost all gone. Embarrassed and angry, the struggling biker yelled out a hoarse "No" while the hovering judge reminded the players that their food could not be shared.

Ten minutes later the confident biker was done with a time of just under thirty minutes. He pushed away from the table and waved to his fans. The other man struggled on but it was obviously hopeless from the looks of the food left on his plate. The contest was over.

The judge leaped on the platform and held the winner's arm aloft in a sign of victory. The two bikers shook hands and the loser skulked off to hoots and jeers. Then the winner asked a waitress to fetch him a doggy bag. When she brought it he reached over and dumped the contents of the defeated biker's steak and trimmings into the sack.

"Once I get back out on that ol' highway this hunk of meat will make me a fine afternoon snack," he said loud enough for all to hear. "Now, tell me what you got for my desert?" ∎

Recipes from Texas

— MARIAN CLARK

Chili, Texas style, is the official state dish. Never have so few ingredients created such a sensation. Chili is a gastronomical wonder-food that comes from humble beginnings yet has achieved almost mythical status. Here is a typical Texas recipe.

Route 66 Chili

2 pounds trimmed beef, cut in small cubes or
    coarsely ground
½ teaspoon hot sauce
1 teaspoon Worcestershire sauce
8 ounces tomato sauce
3 beef bouillon cubes
Water as needed

Cook meat over medium heat in melted shortening until lightly browned. Add hot sauce, Worcestershire sauce, tomato sauce, bouillon cubes, and enough water to barely cover the meat mixture. Cover and simmer for about 45 minutes. Stir occasionally and add water if needed.

Spice Mix:
3 tablespoons chili powder
2 teaspoons cumin
2 tablespoons dried onion flakes
1 tablespoon garlic powder
½ teaspoon salt
½ teaspoon pepper
½ teaspoon oregano
1 bay leaf

Combine spices. Add half of the combined spices, including the bay leaf. Cook an additional hour, adding water as needed. Add remaining spices and continue cooking another 15 minutes. Adjust water to desired thickness. Remove bay leaf and taste to adjust salt and spices.

Note: Cooked pinto beans may be added for the last 15 minutes of cooking time — 4 to 6 cups, or according to personal preference.

Side dishes may include cornbread or tortillas, a green salad, guacamole, and fresh fruit. Beer is most often the Texas drink of choice. 6-8 servings without beans.

"Crocodile" Lile hangs out with sign by Stanley Marsh 3

DELBERT AND RUTH TREW remain driving forces behind the Old Route 66 Association of Texas. From their ranch near Alanreed, the Trews are also active in the Devil's Rope and Old Route 66 Museum and many church and civic endeavors in the McLean and Alanreed area.

A memorial brick from Old Route 66 Museum in McLean

Ruth Trew's Chocolate Zucchini Cake

2 eggs
½ cup soft margarine
½ cup oil
1¾ cups sugar
4 tablespoons cocoa
1 teaspoon vanilla
1 teaspoon soda
1 teaspoon cinnamon
½ teaspoon cloves
½ cup sour milk
2½ cups flour
2 cups finely chopped zucchini
¼ cup chocolate chips

Mix together all ingredients except zucchini and chocolate chips. Stir zucchini into batter last. Pour cake batter into greased and floured 9x13-inch cake pan. Sprinkle chocolate chips on top. Bake in preheated 325 degree oven for 45-50 minutes. Needs no icing. 12 servings.

THE ROUTE 66 STEAKHOUSE IN GROOM is a great biker stop. Will Frost now runs this eatery that many remember as the Golden Spread Grill. Rubye Denton bought the grill in 1957 and presided over it until her retirement.

Matthias Guenther, Harley biker from Kleinmachnow, Germany, says he had his best steak on Route 66 at this location. He also enjoyed the live music and friendly service.

Here is a place where travelers often find a piece of the real west. Local cowboys regularly pull up in the parking lot with their horses in trailers behind the pickups. They come in after shaking dust from hats and chaps and are careful not to tangle spurs with the furniture. Photograph sessions are common.

Squash Casserole
GOLDEN SPREAD GRILL

3½ pounds yellow squash, trimmed and sliced
½ cup green pepper
1 large onion, diced
2 ripe tomatoes, chopped
8 tablespoons margarine or butter
4 eggs
½ cup sugar
1½ teaspoons salt

¼ teaspoon pepper
¼ pound ham, diced
¾ cup grated cheddar cheese
¾ cup crushed potato chips for topping

Combine squash, pepper, onion, and tomatoes in a large saucepan. Add a small amount of water, cover and cook until tender, about 20-30 minutes, stirring occasionally to mash the squash. Drain thoroughly in a colander.

Add all remaining ingredients except chips. Pour mixture into a 9x12-inch lightly greased casserole and top with the crushed chips. Bake uncovered in a preheated 350 degree oven for 30-45 minutes until top is golden brown. 10-12 servings.

AUTHENTIC RANCHERS AND COWHANDS greet guests at the 7,000-acre Figure 3 Ranch each morning during the summer as the sun rises across the flat countryside. Wagons transport guests to the rim of Palo Duro Canyon where the scenery itself is worth the trip. A breathtaking view awaits as early morning mist rises from the canyon that drops some 700-800 feet below the frying-pan flat land. Stories come naturally and the food is belly-filling good. Sausage is spicy and the gravy is rich. Scrambled eggs come from the Dutch oven in golden mounds and tasty biscuits can be painted with butter or hidden under satisfying gravy. Authentic cowboy coffee completes the feast.

Hosts are Tom and Anne Christian and their cowhands, who see that every gathering is completed with a cow-chip throwing contest. If you miss breakfast, check out the Cowboy Evening Dinners, complete with man-sized steaks and giant burgers. This is a genuine Texas *experience*.

Cowboy Morning Sourdough Biscuits
FIGURE 3 RANCH

5 cups flour
1 teaspoon sugar
1 teaspoon baking soda
½ teaspoon salt
¼ cup cooking oil
2½ cups sourdough starter

Place flour in a large bowl and make a well in the flour. Pour starter into the well and add all the other ingredients. Stir until mixture no longer picks up flour. Cover and let rise three to four hours, or overnight. Place dough on floured board and roll to ½-inch thickness. Cut out biscuits and place in greased 18-inch cast-iron Dutch oven. Set by the campfire to rise for 1-2 hours. Place hot lid on oven, set oven on coals, and place coals on lid. Cook until browned, 5-8 minutes. 15 biscuits.

Sourdough Starter:
4 medium baking potatoes, peeled and quartered
4½ cups water
1 cup all purpose flour
2 teaspoons sugar
½ teaspoon salt

Place potatoes and water in medium saucepan. Cover and boil until potatoes are done, about 30 minutes. Drain liquid into measuring cup. (Do not use potatoes.) Measure 2½ cups of the potato water into large mixing bowl. Add flour, sugar and salt. Stir well. Cover with cheesecloth and let stand at room temperature until starter begins to bubble, about 4 days. Place in covered plastic container in refrigerator.

To use, take 2½ cups of starter out for above biscuit recipe. To remaining starter, add 1½ cups flour and 1½ cups warm water. Let starter stand at room temperature overnight, then replace lid and return to refrigerator. Use regularly and enjoy! Note: Some cooks like to add 1 package of dry yeast to the original starter to give it an extra boost. If this is done, the starter will begin to bubble in 2 days.

From Trond Moberg's notebook

"Usually a couple of us sign up to eat the 72-ounce steak at the Big Texan. This is one of our favorite places; the motel is great and the hospitality/service is superb. We are almost halfway along 66 by now and so we party late. We don't start again the next morning until 10:30. Next year we will have Hody Porterfield prepare his special campfire breakfast outdoors for us."

"Texas Caviar"

Route 66 Big Texan

2 cans (16 ounce each) black-eyed peas, drained
1 medium jalapeño, minced and seeded
¼ small white onion, chopped
⅓ cup Italian dressing
½ green pepper, chopped
1 tablespoon seasoned salt
2 tablespoons chili powder
2 tablespoons ground cumin
¼ teaspoon ground red pepper

Combine black-eyed peas with remaining ingredients. Serve chilled with corn chips.

    5 cups

Cafes, bars, antique shops, galleries, and a collection of old businesses line the historic San Jacinto District on Sixth Street, Route 66, in Amarillo. This thirteen block segment of the historic highway was inducted into the National Register of Historic Places in October of 1994.

The street is pure Route 66. The Golden Light Cafe, the oldest restaurant in Amarillo operating in the same location, can be found here—try the burgers!

Amarillo businessmen joined forces several years ago to put together a book of favorite food as a benefit for the Fine Arts Division of Amarillo College. Hidden behind the red bandanna cover are some real jewels that not only satisfy the palate but reflect a Texas-size sense of humor!

Hot Damn Texas Panhandle Salami

Cookin' with Amarillo's Corporate Cowboys
Ben Konis

2 pounds lean chopped meat
2 tablespoons Morton's Tenderquick
1½ teaspoons liquid smoke
¼ teaspoon each of garlic powder and onion powder
1 cup cold water
Scant teaspoon peppercorns

Mix all ingredients well. Shape into two tight rolls, wrap in waxed paper and refrigerate for 24 hours. Remove wrap and bake salami on cookie sheet in preheated 225 degree oven for 2 hours.

(My mother-in-law, Rosie, gave me this secret salami recipe. Great eating with rye bread, Dijon mustard, and a beer with ice and lime.)

Cookin' with Amarillo's Corporate Cowboys

Cream Cheese with Horseradish Sauce
W. E. Juett

1 (16-ounce) jar apple jelly
1 (18-ounce) jar apricot-pineapple preserves
1 (1½-ounce) can dry mustard
1 (5-ounce) jar creamed horseradish
1 (8-ounce) block of cream cheese

Mix all ingredients. Spoon generously over cream cheese.

    Serve on a platter with a cheese knife and assorted crackers.

    Unused sauce can be stored in refrigerator, covered, for up to two months.

Chicken-Fried Steak and Gravy

Cookin' with Amarillo's Corporate Cowboys
Carlton Clemens

Select 1 pound round steak or cutlet of desired thickness. Cut into four servings. Pound with meat tenderizer (cleaver) or edge of small plate. Cover with flour and dust off excess. Dip slices in wash made of ½ milk and ½ buttermilk. Replace in flour and dust off excess. Deep fry at 350 degrees until the steak floats. Continue by pan frying at 300 degrees until meat is browned on both sides. Serve hot with gravy.

To make the gravy, combine equal parts of flour and vegetable oil. In a heavy skillet, heat the oil until hot — about 300 degrees. Add the flour, stirring carefully so the mixture doesn't stick to the pan. When the oil and flour mixture is hot, add milk and continue to cook until desired thickness is reached. Salt and pepper to taste.

Wild Plum Jelly from the Frying Pan Ranch

(Recipe for Husbands)
Cookin' with Amarillo's Corporate Cowboys
Stanley Marsh 3

Approach house carefully. Do not disturb any workers, paid or volunteer, who are moving around strange contraptions, pans and containers.

Expect to find all edible food out in small refrigerator near bedroom, in cans, or in the cupboards. Refrigerators are full of berries.

Be careful when you get up in the middle of the night not to jiggle any pans on the stove, island, or countertops, because they may be brimming full of plum juice in one stage of jell or another.

Do not be alarmed when your wife jumps up out of bed or out of the bathtub at various times and runs in the kitchen, moving about containers.

Do not ask the cowboys why they have coolers full of berries sunning in the front yard. They are ripening. You would just look foolish.

Smile and enjoy it. It's a beautiful harvest. The jelly tastes great and you will get a lot of compliments for just having stayed out of the way.

P.S. Bring your wife ice water or snacks; at night take her for a ride or to the movie on the weekend. She is tired from being on her feet. Let her choose the TV show. Encourage her to rest.

FORMER AMARILLO RESIDENT, DONNA LEA, travels Route 66 at every opportunity and swears bikers can't help but develop a craving for "buffalo chips." Once tried, they'll become a staple in every saddle-bag.

Donna Lea's Buffalo Chips

2 cups brown sugar
2 cups granulated sugar
2 cups margarine
4 eggs
4 cups flour
2 teaspoons baking powder
2 teaspoons soda
½ teaspoon salt
2 cups corn flakes
2 cups oatmeal
1 6-ounce package chocolate or butterscotch chips
1 7-ounce package coconut
1 cup raisins
1 cup pecans, peanuts or mixed nuts

Prepare these cookies in a very large mixing bowl or a roaster pan. Cream margarine with sugar and eggs. Stir in flour, baking powder, soda, and salt. Add remaining ingredients and blend well. Use an ice cream scoop to dip mixture. Place cookies on greased cookie sheet and flatten slightly, allowing space for cookies to spread.

Cookies will be 3 to 4 inches in size. Bake in pre-heated 350 degree oven for 15 to 18 minutes.

Approximately 48 large cookies.

Note: Many variations work well with these cookies. Try other cereals instead of corn flakes. Substitute dried banana for raisins or use ¼ cup applesauce to replace an equal part of the oil, use M&M candies in place of chips; add more raisins if desired, and include seeds or other dried fruit for added flavor.

LIFE CAN'T GET ANY BETTER then when bikers take to the open road in the Texas panhandle. Space abounds, the highway leads, and the majesty of America takes over. The sky, the clouds, the wind at your back, mirages, a distant rain, lightening on the Llano Estacado — it is Route 66 at its best!

Just beware of those 18-wheelers and the ever-present wind.

Bob's Tenderloin

Cookin' with Amarillo Corporate Cowboys
Mansfield Cattle Company, Vega

1 beef tenderloin, about 5-6 pounds, well trimmed

Marinade:

⅔ cup soy sauce
1 cup orange juice

Several shakes Worcestershire Sauce
4 teaspoons vinegar
Juice of one lemon
Pinch of sugar
Garlic and pepper to taste

Combine and mix all marinade ingredients together. Marinate tenderloin for several hours, turning occasionally. Cook on charcoal grill over medium coals (about 6 inches above coals) for 30 to 45 minutes. Tenderloin should be mopped with marinade and turned about 3 times.

LANDERGEN IS NO MORE. George and Melba Rook brought the old truck stop to life again in 1996 in time for the first major 66 gathering, "Run to the Heartland." With George's declining health, they closed the doors of their Neon Soda Saloon in March of 1998, but many remember the scrumptious biscuits Melba served there.

Melba Rook's Buttermilk Biscuits

4 cups flour
1 teaspoon salt
¼ cup baking powder
¼ cup sugar
⅔ cup butter
1⅓ cup buttermilk

Sift together the flour, salt, baking powder, and sugar. Cut in the butter and add milk, forming a soft dough. Knead on a floured board. Roll out to ¾-1-inch depth. Cut into 1½-inch circles and place an inch apart on a greased sheet. Bake in a preheated 400 degree oven for 10-12 minutes. 2 dozen biscuits.

From Trond Moberg's notebook

"Mid-Point Cafe and we are half way. Fran and her crew greet us with a fabulous lunch and apple pie. We recommend the grilled ham and cheese. This is a special place and also one of the highlights; we feel welcome. The Route 66 gift shop has a very good selection of merchandise. We spend a couple of hours here with splendid food, very nice people, and photo sessions at the Midway sign."

THE MID-POINT CAFE (ADRIAN CAFE), caught at the geo-mathematical center of Route 66, is the oldest continuously operating eatery along Route 66 between Amarillo and Tucumcari. A sign out front proclaims: Mid-Point Cafe, 1,139 miles to Chicago and 1,139 to Los Angeles.

Fran Houser owns the eatery that has been home to locals for years. Joann Harwell is often there baking her famous "ugly crust pies." Fran says this coconut cream Pie is close to the one prepared by former owner Jesse Finch, a legendary Route 66 figure.

Coconut Cream Pie
Mid-Point Cafe

⅔ cups sugar
2½ tablespoons cornstarch
½ teaspoon salt
1 tablespoon flour
3 cups milk
3 egg yolks, beaten
1 tablespoon butter
¾ cup coconut
1½ teaspoons vanilla

Mix sugar, cornstarch, salt and flour well. Stir in milk gradually. Cook over medium heat, stirring constantly until mixture is hot; stir in beaten egg yolks. Cook until thick. Add butter, coconut, and vanilla. Pour into a 9-inch pie shell and top with meringue. Bake in a preheated 400 degree oven for 8-10 minutes.

Meringue:
3 egg whites, beaten
6 tablespoons sugar
¼ teaspoon cream of tartar
½ teaspoon vanilla

Combine and cover the pie. Bake as directed above.

It was just after Christmas, 2000, when Joann Harwell of Vega shared a story that represents the very best of the holiday spirit along Route 66. She said, "There was a severe storm predicted here for Christmas Day. I had worked for Fran at the Midpoint on Christmas Eve and she was playing with the idea of staying open for Christmas Day to catch stranded travelers should the storm develop. I volunteered to help but when I got up Christmas morning, the roads were already too slick for me to get to Adrian.

"Sure enough, people started pulling into Adrian by Christmas afternoon to wait out the storm. By that time, Fran had prepared potato soup, chili, stew, and loads of cornbread, along with several cakes and cobblers. Instead of taking advantage of other's troubles, Miss Fran set out the dishes, formed a buffet line, and fed everyone who came through her door free of charge. The hotel in Adrian filled up and some people spent the night at the community center, so she sent stew, cornbread, and coffee over there as well.

"Fran reported this was the best Christmas ever for her. She and her Christmas family had an absolutely wonderful time."

Joann concluded, "Fran gave of her heart, and I feel so proud to know that goodness still reigns on the road."

LEAVE TEXAS AMID THE GLENRIO GHOSTS who preside under the very dilapidated Last Motel in Texas/First Motel in Texas sign. ■

Butt Darts

— MICHAEL WALLIS

If you are ever cruising Route 66 and happen to find refuge in a saloon where a butt darts contest is underway consider yourself lucky and stay put. Call it a day and don't go any farther. Pull up a chair or stool and allow your bike to cool down. Do not leave until a winner has been declared.

Although it is played in bars and other venues around the nation, the best place to witness a butt dart game is out on the Mother Road with plenty of cold beverages and lots of good pub chow like pickled pigs feet, hard boiled eggs, and beer nuts.

The game is simple enough. Basic butt darts calls for a player to insert a quarter between the cheeks of the buttocks (fully clothed), waddle about 15 feet to a small container on the floor, and release the coin with hopes of it dropping into the container. The individual, or the team if you're playing teams, with the most direct hits wins. May sound simple enough but try it while wearing tight jeans or leather riding britches and you'll find out just how hard it is.

Sometimes coffee or beer mugs are used for the catching vessels but the best butt darters, like the ones we've witnessed playing the game on Route 66 in Texas and points west, prefer to use a whiskey shot glass.

Some bikers claim that they've seen advanced butt darts, sometimes called flaming butt darts, played. This involves dropping candles — both lit and then unlit — from the player's derriere into a container. You earn one point if the candle enters the cup and the flame goes out and two points if the wick stays lit. If players are able to contort their bodies, they are allowed to cup their hands around the flame while moving toward the container. Usually the same candle is used for all rounds so the longer the game goes on the shorter the candle gets.

A story still makes the rounds of bike shops, barbershops and cafes up and down the old highway about a legendary butt dart contest held one evening in a Texas panhandle beer joint. Some top notch butt darters were competing when the door swung open and in walked a Lone Star belle with piled cotton candy hair, big blue eyes, and legs that stretched clear to Dallas. She wore hot pink shorts, bone white go-go boots, and a halter-top so scanty it made the bouncer blush.

This little gal proceeded to put some folding money on the bar in exchange for a roll of new quarters. Then she peeled off the paper and slapped that entire roll of coins where the sun doesn't shine. Proud as punch, she sashayed toward that glass jigger and when she was straddling the target she cut loose with her load. The sound of quarters spitting into that glass sounded like a slot machine paying off. Not a coin missed the mark.

It was quiet as a country graveyard in that joint when the woman pranced to the bar and picked up the winner's kitty stashed in a coffee can formerly used as a catch container for novice butt darters in training. She flashed her best smile and walked to the door. Before she left, she turned to a stunned cowboy biker sitting at a table with his mouth open and just a dribble of spit hanging on his lower lip. She flipped him a bright shiny quarter and flashed a wink. Then she was gone.

I've never found a soul who was actually there that night but I'd like to think its all true. Of course, I believe that jackalopes exist and my mind is still open to the exact whereabouts of Elvis.

Still, there is always a chance that some cool evening out on Route 66, while you are telling lies to a table of fellow bikers, the door may open and that Queen of the Darters will appear. Keep hope alive. ∎

Biker Flicks

Most bikers polled consistently select *Easy Rider*, the 1969 film starring Peter Fonda, Dennis Hopper, and Jack Nicholson, as the ultimate biker movie of all time. A distant second place finisher is the *Wild One*, the 1954 release with Marlon Brando, riding a Triumph, not a Harley. Here's a starter list of flicks to check out.

Easy Rider
The Wild One
Electra Glide In Blue
Hells Angels On Wheels
Mad Max
The Wild Angels
Black Rain
Running Cool
C. C. & Company
Born to Ride
Knightriders
Harley-Davidson and the Marlboro Man

Sell Sell Sell

— MICHAEL WALLIS

When folks complain that Route 66 is getting too commercial, I have to laugh. The highway has always been a corridor of commerce for people trying to make a living — selling a room for the night, a tankful of gas, some postcards, a peek inside the snake pit, a meat loaf sandwich. That's what the highway is all about — people serving other people.

Whenever you visit one of the countless Route 66 attractions, pause at a motel, or dine at one of the classic greasy spoons, plan on meeting honest-to-goodness people, interested in you and the world around them.

When you step inside a genuine Route 66 cafe, look for lumps in the mashed potatoes and expect the waitresses to have coffeepots welded to their fists. The only thing instant will be the service.

Along Route 66, folks have always known how to turn a buck. Travel a few miles. You'll find the odyssey is worth every penny. But bikers beware — you will also find that you will be shipping lots of road souvenirs home. ■

New Mexico

Fast facts from New Mexico

- Route 66 mileage in New Mexico — 261

- Santa Fe is the oldest government seat in the United States.

- Official New Mexico vegetables are chiles and frijoles even though the chile is technically classified as a fruit. The state cookie is the biscochito.

- Tortillas, served in abundance in New Mexico, are the fastest growing segment of the baking industry.

- Original Route 66 (Santa Fe to Los Lunas) and the post-1936 alignments of Route 66 cross in downtown Albuquerque, the only place the Mother Road crosses itself.

New Mexico Biker Road Rules

- Safety Helmet, required by law under age of 18

- Eye Protection, required by law unless equipped with windscreen

Must see in New Mexico

- State Line to San Jon — The 20 mile stretch of original Route 66 between Glenrio and San Jon is a test of Harley independence and not recommended by experienced riders.

- Tucumcari — The Caprock Amphitheater Summer Musical Production of *Billy the Kid* is located outdoors on the bluff of the Llano Estacado, 10 miles south on NM 469.

- Santa Rosa — Blue Hole — this clear artesian spring is 87 feet deep - an amazing stop that is highly recommended by bikers.

- La Pradira Lane Scenic Drive — Take SR 91 for 10 miles south of Santa Rosa to Puerto de Luna where Coronado once camped, then head toward Dilla to a bar and refreshments.

- Santa Fe — On the old alignment, a city unlike any other. Explore and enjoy, but remember parking may be a problem.

- Bernalillo — Bike the Jemez Mountain Trail Drive for a day of spectacular beauty.

Part of the original Route 66 between Glenrio and San Jon

The Land of Enchantment

NEW MEXICO

★ Santa Fe

● Albuquerque

66

- ALBUQUERQUE
  - Drive Central Avenue, an 18-mile ode to Route 66 history that includes the Kimo Theater and the De Anza and El Vado Motels.
  - Enjoy the International Balloon Festival for nine days each October.
  - Visit Old Town, 2000 block of Central Avenue NW, then one block north.
  - Ride Sandia Peak Aerial Tramway, 11704 Coronado NE.

- LOS LUNAS — From Los Lunas, take NM 6, historic Route 66, for 33 miles to Correo, a great biker drive.

- GRANTS
  - See Ice Caves and Bandera Crater, twenty-five minutes southwest on SR 53.
  - View Pueblo of Acoma, the oldest continuously inhabited city in the United States. Twenty minutes east of Grants on I-40, take exit 102 south.

Beacons in the Dark

- TUCUMCARI — BLUE SWALLOW MOTEL
  815 East Tucumcari Boulevard

- SANTA FE — EL REY INN
  1862 Cerrillos Road

Mural in Tucumcari

- *Albuquerque* — Best Western American Motor Inn (Trond Moberg suggests this for large biker group) 12999 Central NE

- *GALLUP* — EL RANCHO HOTEL AND MOTEL 1000 East 66 Avenue

El Rancho Hotel, Gallup

Where to buy stuff in New Mexico

- *TUCUMCARI* — TeePee Curios, across the street from the Blue Swallow

- *CLINES CORNER* — A giant collection of velvet paintings, rattlesnake ashtrays, and rubber tomahawks that has lured motorists since 1934

- *CUBERO* — Meet Lucy and Lawrence Peterson at their small store and saloon.

- *BLUEWATER* — Route 66 Swap Meet. Rated by some bikers as the best swap meet on Route 66. Eighty-nine year old Thomas Lamance has a motto: "Open when I feel like it, or by appointment."

- *GALLUP* — Richardson's Trading Post

Swap Meet 66, Bluewater

Favorite hangouts for food and drink

- *TUCUMCARI*
  - *DEL'S RESTAURANT*, 1202 Tucumcari East Boulevard. Good food in Tucumcari since the early 1940s
  - *LA CITA*, 812 S. 1st Street. Eat under a Mexican sombrero!

Near Tucumcari

- SANTA ROSA —
  - JOE'S BAR AND GRILL, 865 Will Rogers Drive. On Route 66 since 1956
  - LAKE CITY DINER, 101 4th Street

Santa Fe

- SANTA FE
  - TIA SOFIA'S (especially for breakfast), 210 W. San Francisco
  - THE SHED, 113 East Palace
  - BOBCAT BITE, southeast of Santa Fe on the original 66 alignment. Highly recommended
  - ROUTE 66 SANDWICH COMPANY, 2430 Cerrillos Road

Bobcat Bite, Santa Fe

- BERNALILLO
  - SILVA SALOON, Camino Del Pueblo (Old Route 66). Open since 1933 and still operating with the 3rd liquor license issued in New Mexico
  - RANGE CAFE, 925 Camino del Pueblo

- MORIARTY — El Comedor de Anayas, West Route 66 Avenue. A long-time local favorite

- ALBUQUERQUE
  - M & J RESTAURANT / SANITARY TORTILLA FACTORY, 403 2nd Street SW. A place not to be missed
  - FRONTIER RESTAURANT, 2400 Central NE. A longtime Route 66 and university favorite
  - LINDY'S, 500 Central SW. Steve Vatoseow runs this historic Route 66 eatery across from the Kimo Theater.
  - THE ROUTE 66 DINER, 1405 Central Avenue SE

Marlo Strehlow Archer at the Route 66 Diner, Albuquerque

- GRANTS — URANIUM CAFE, 519 W. SANTA FE

- GALLUP
  - EARL'S FAMILY RESTAURANT, 1400 East Hwy. 66. Serving Route 66 customers since 1947
  - RANCH KITCHEN, 3001 Route 66 West. Over forty years on Route 66

Glenrio

— MICHAEL WALLIS

"Sometimes it's a little better to travel than arrive."
— *Zen and the Art of Motorcycle Maintenance*

The sun is coming to life on old Route 66 in Glenrio, a wind-swept town straddling the border of New Mexico and Texas. I have come on my Harley with a few other rider pals to pay our respects and snoop around. We park our bikes and hunker down on the edge of the frayed highway and watch as regiments of ants — just starting the day shift — construct cone-shaped mounds with bits of earth, sand, and grains of asphalt and concrete. These days only the ants can make a living off Route 66 in Glenrio.

Once a bustling railroad hamlet and later a noteworthy stopping place on America's Main Street, Glenrio was left high and dry years ago when Interstate 40 — the super slab — bypassed the place, forcing businesses to close and people to move on. It is now a ghost town in the making. Not that Glenrio was ever a metropolis. Even at its peak during the heyday of Route 66, the town was only a cluster of stores, cafes, filling stations, and frame houses with a population of less than one hundred. It seemed much larger because of the constant stream of tourists and truckers who paused for a hot meal, cold drink, tank of gas, or a bed for the night.

Glenrio used to be as busy as a noontime greasy spoon. Starting out as a farming community around 1905, by the next year a railroad station was established and the community bustled with cattle and freight ship-

ments. From 1910 until 1934 the border town prospered and even supported a newspaper, the Glenrio *Tribune*. By 1920, six years before the birth of Route 66, Glenrio had a hotel, a hardware store, and a land office. When John Ford made *The Grapes of Wrath* into a motion picture in 1940, some scenes were shot at Glenrio.

The glory times are long gone. Nowadays more dogs than people live here. The town straddling two states has evolved into an oasis for tumbleweeds and roadrunners on the prowl for reptile suppers.

In spite of that travelers, including a fair number of bikers, still pause to pay their respects. They reflect on what it must have been like when the State Line Bar sold whiskey, beer, and gasoline and the Little Juarez Diner and the First in Texas/Last In Texas Motel and Cafe were humming — back when life in Glenrio was sweeter than truck stop pie. Back before grass poked through the pavement. Back before buildings turned into derelicts and the ghosts moved in.

I do not mind the ghosts. Most are old friends. That is why I come to Glenrio and to other towns along the Mother Road that time has forgotten. To me these places are as important as the many Route 66 towns that are still perking and serving up hospitality to generations of new travelers. The ghost places where deserted buildings with no doors or windows stare at the varicose highway, help remind me of the way life used to be before much of the nation became generic. I also like Glenrio because I can stand on the border in two time zones with one foot in the Lone Star State and the other in the Land of Enchantment.

Then, too, there is always road treasure. Stained menus from a cafe and yellowed gas receipts blow through the weeds. Broken coffee mugs, bottle caps, and dead spark plugs hide in the dust. In the past I have found a trucker's daily logbook, ceramic shards of bygone times, and newspapers as old as me.

On this day at Glenrio with my biker friends, I once again went hunting for remnants from the past. I found what I was looking for just inside a row of empty tourist cabins. Crammed inside an envelope were cancelled checks. The checks were imprinted,

TEXAS LONGHORN
ON HIGHWAY 66
FIRST AND LAST STOP IN TEXAS
GLENRIO, NEW MEXICO

The checks were dated in the 1960s and the 1970s, back when I recalled coming through Glenrio as a hitchhiking Marine toting a seabag. I recall the town was bright and shining late at night as all kinds of people — tourists, salesmen, truckers, and servicemen — stopped to refuel themselves and their vehicles.

Homer Ehresman signed the checks I held. I remembered him too. Back during the glory times of the Mother Road he owned and operated various businesses in town including a service station, cafe, and a tourist court. His wife also ran the post office. My friend Delbert Trew, a Texas panhandle rancher, told me that when he and his dad passed Glenrio they always stopped to have some of Mrs. Ehresman's wonderful pie. Delbert said it got to the point that when they walked in the cafe the waitress just smiled, cut a coconut cream pie in half and placed the halves before the two men. I also remember that pie and how good it tasted washed down with ice water and coffee.

The Ehresmans were there in Glenrio when the road was being paved in the 1930s. The workers slept in tents alongside the road and they made thirty cents an hour. Homer and his wife fed the highway crews three meals a day — all they could eat, family-style — for a dollar. During the bad times when flocks of Okies and Dust Bowl pilgrims came through town, the Ehresmans never turned anyone away from their cafe even if they had no money. Occasionally

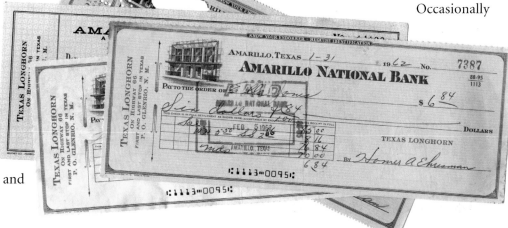

destitute diners even came back to Glenrio when they got on their feet and paid what they owed.

And now here I am, standing in the remains of Glenrio, clutching Mr. Ehresman's checks. They were made out to meat companies, a firm that repaired the ice machine, and various other vendors and suppliers that kept his place humming. I thumbed through the stack of checks and then I reached the real treasure — the payroll checks. They were made out to the waitresses and some were advance salary checks to tide the women over. I read the names on the checks — Alice Davis, Dora May Campbell, Ella Jones, Midred Harris and many others.

They had been real waitresses. They served the public and never walked up to a customer and told them their name. You knew damn good and well she was a waitress. Her feet hurt, she yelled at the cook, and called everybody Honey.

I wondered what had become of these waitresses over the past forty years. I knew many of them had died and moved on when the interstate came along in the 1970s, cut off the whole town and left it to die. I showed the other bikers what I had found and gave them each a check to keep as a souvenir of this stop. I put the rest of the checks inside my leather jacket and then we went to our bikes. A raven started squawking from a Chinese elm as we took our leave.

I still have those Glenrio checks. They are with my other cherished remnants from the old road. I value them and know that they are the DNA of Route 66. They spark memories and help me understand what needs to be done to prevent more ghost places from appearing. ∎

Old Familiar Places

— MICHAEL WALLIS

In Tucumcari I can really take the pulse of Route 66 at Teepee Curios and the Blue Swallow Motel. When I call on both of these biker-friendly highway icons I find the beat of the Mother Road is strong and steady in New Mexico. I know in my heart that the much-heralded revival of interest in Route 66 is as real as the road itself.

To prove it to myself, all I need do is look into the eyes of Mike and Betty Callens, the steadfast proprietors of the Teepee since 1985, four years after I-40 bypassed Tucumcari. Instead of allowing the highway bypass to cripple their town, the Callens and other Tucumcari citizens pitched in and helped build an economy based on tourism and local trade.

Mike and Betty Callens are survivors. They are as resilient as the old highway outside their shop's front door. They are also inspiring role models for some Route 66 newcomers who have taken over the nearby Blue Swallow Motel.

When I enter the lobby of the motel, a Route 66 fixture since 1939, I still feel the presence of Lillian Redman, the former Harvey Girl and an authentic road angel who owned and operated this historic property for so many years. Miss Lillian, as we called her, was born in Clifton, Texas, and came to New Mexico with her family in a covered wagon in 1915. She moved to Tucumcari in 1923 and after finishing school she worked as a legal secretary and later in the famous Harvey House restaurants in Kingman and Winslow. During the 1940s she owned and operated a restaurant in Gallup before coming home to Tucumcari to work as a chef.

In 1958, Lillian was given the Blue Swallow as a wedding present by her fiancée Floyd Redman. Lillian added the office, an apartment for her aging parents, and the giant neon sign that transformed the Blue Swallow into a Mother Road icon. Floyd died in 1973, but Lillian stuck it out on the old highway through good times and bad until she just wore out.

Blue Swallow Motel, Tucumcari

Lillian passed away in 1999, just shy of her ninetieth birthday. Before she left us, Lillian and her magical cat Smoky, moved into a small house not too far from the Blue Swallow. Sometimes she returned to visit her beloved motel. She liked to sit in the lobby and greet guests. She died knowing the Blue Swallow ended up in caring hands.

Hilda and Dale Bakke now own and operate the Blue Swallow. The Bakkes and their teenage daughter moved to Tucumcari from Colorado and took over the declining motel in 1998 after Dale spotted a newspaper advertisement offering what was described as "The Deal of the Century." Neither of the Bakkes knew much about Tucumcari, motel management, or Route 66. They became quick studies.

"We thought it had great potential," Dale told me. "We liked the style of architecture, the neon, and the good feeling about the place. We also saw a great deal of restoration work had to be done."

Hilda and Dale rolled up their sleeves and went to work. They scrubbed and painted, stripped the wooden floors, updated the plumbing and electricity, and always "tried to repair rather than replace." Dale, a skilled electrician by trade, lovingly rebuilt the neon blue birds outside the rooms and restored the Blue Swallow's blinking signature sign that has acted as the old road's night light and attracted weary voyagers for decades. The Bakkes' cat, Frances, naps curled up on a lobby chair where she is often mistaken for Smoky. Two photo portraits of a smiling Miss Lillian have places of honor on a lobby wall.

"We have great respect for Lillian Redman and what she did day in and day out for so many years," Dale tells me. His words make my day and also bring back other memories

like the day a collection of Harley bikers from around the world staged a very special parade for Miss Lillian.

It was in June of 1996 when the largest group of Harley motorcycles and riders ever assembled at one time, journeyed the length of the entire highway. It would be the first of two historic tours my wife, Suzanne, and I would be asked to lead for the Harley Owners Group (H.O.G.). I knew virtually nothing about motorcycles and so we made the trip in a van done up in Harley colors and Route 66 decals.

Many days into the westward trek the bikers crossed into New Mexico and spent the night in Tucumcari, the smallest city to host us during the two-week tour. The local officials planned a bike parade and all the riders cued up on the large parking at the city's new convention center. State policemen and town cops were out in full

Michael Wallis rides to see Miss Lillian behind Kent Meacham and becomes a born-again biker, Tucumcari

force to guide us and keep order. The streets, especially Route 66, were lined with eager spectators anxious to see the Harleys strut their stuff.

At the very last minute as we prepared to lead off in our van, I learned that for unexplained reasons the parade route had been altered and now we would not be taking all of the Mother Road through town. This meant we would not be passing The Blue Swallow and Miss Lillian who waited outside in her wheelchair. The bikers had heard about Lillian and her motel at a tour seminar that we conducted so they were anxious to honor her.

I was furious but it was too late. The signal was given and off we went. Later when it became clear that we were on an abbreviated route, I could see in my mirror that some of the bikers behind us appeared confused. By the time the procession returned to the staging grounds at the convention center, I was surrounded by a swarm of bikers questioning me about how the Blue Swallow had been bypassed. I told them what I knew but that was obviously not going to do.

Several bikers held a hasty conference and despite standing police orders forbidding any more parades, they quickly pulled together their forces and formed a convoy of a couple of hundred bikes. Suzanne jumped on the back of one bike and I climbed behind Kent Meacham, a stalwart biker and true Road Warrior in every sense. We took off, passing the bewildered police and headed straight to the Blue Swallow.

When we slowly passed in review, our horns blaring and arms pumping, a beaming Miss Lillian waved back and blew kisses. It was a tremendous salute to a great lady and one of the old road's most loyal protectors.

Tears rolled down my cheeks. It was at that moment — on Kent's bike before Miss Lillian and that old neon palace — I decided that I was going to get a Harley. It was crystal clear in my mind.

Miss Lillian at the Blue Swallow, Tucumcari

Later that evening we went back to the Blue Swallow and visited with Lillian. It was a fine time with bikers galore filling the small lobby. I recall her last words to Suzanne as we prepared to leave. When she saw tears on Suzanne's cheeks, Lillian asked what was wrong and Suzanne told her she just hated saying goodbye and not knowing when or if she would see her again. Lillian smiled and said, "Don't cry. Don't you know I'll always be here? I'll always see you in all the old familiar places."

As usual Miss Lillian was right. We still do and always will. ■

Note: Shortly after the 1996 tour ended, Michael purchased a new Heritage Softtail. He rode it on the next Route 66 tour.

The Freedom of the Open Road

—MARIAN CLARK

German riders Matthias Guenther and Christina Hey spent the last week of August, 2003, in Milwaukee at the 100th Birthday Celebration of Harley-Davidson.

Their American dream trip had only begun. By September 2, they were back at Chicago O'Hare where they picked up the Harleys they had shipped from home.

Christina and Matthias in Chicago as their Route 66 adventure begins

That day, they officially headed down Route 66 for a month of adventure on America's most famous highway.

Christina rides a customized Harley-Davidson Sportster, Model 1998, and Matthias owns a Harley-Davidson Dyna Super Glide, Model 2000. Matthias wrote after returning home to Kleinmachnow, near Berlin, "At the end of September we arrived in Santa Monica. We felt very well because we did it! Before 1989 this kind of adventure was impossible for people from Eastern Germany. More than 2,200 miles on our bikes — it was a great experience for both of us, especially to meet so many lovely people! We remember often the days we spent on Route 66."

Matthias and Christina prepared well and recorded hundreds of road icons on film as they explored the highway. Matthias listed several stops as especially memorable

First, he and Christina met Dixie Lee Evans, the aging queen of burlesque who presides over the Exotic World Museum in Helendale, California. For them, this was the most interesting museum along Route 66 because of the glimpse into the American movie and burlesque industry. Dixie was a Marilyn Monroe impersonator when she was in burlesque.

Dixie Lee Evans, Exotic World Museum, Helendale, California

Nearby, they thoroughly enjoyed the Route 66 bottle trees. This unique attraction resulted from Miles Mahan's desert dream. Mahan moved to the area near Helendale, California, in the 1950s and gradually began collecting bottles. His outdoor "museum" was later named "Hula Ville" for the giant dancer who graced the entrance to his collection. Mahan is gone now, as is the giant hula girl, but the bottle trees he and his friends collected still grace the old plot. The trees are made of bottles, hung on nails driven into posts. Miles and his friends didn't have any way of disposing of them, so the end result still shines in the desert sky.

In Newberry Springs, Matthias and Christina stopped at the Bagdad Cafe where they met the owner, Andrea Pruett. American's think of this stop as the film location for *Bagdad Cafe*. Matthias and Christina had seen the German version of the same film, only with another title, *Out of Rosenheim*, directed by Percy and Eleonore Adlon with Marianne Saegebrecht in the leading role. A biker who had played a bit part in that film happened to be at the cafe when Matthias and Christina were there — a real thrill. Matthias liked the sense of family at the Bagdad Cafe, the lighthearted jokes, good food, and fair prices.

Miles Mahan's bottle trees, near Helendale, California

Bagdad Cafe, Newberry Springs, California

In Cubero, New Mexico, they met and enjoyed visiting with Lucy and Lawrence Peterson in their small store and saloon. In Bluewater, they got acquainted with 89-year-old Thomas Lamance at his 66 Swap Meet. The swap meet was a favorite stop that Matthias recommends for all bikers. He especially liked the sign, "Open when I feel like it or by appointment."

Thomas Lamance at his 66 Swap Meet in Cubero, New Mexico

Halltown, Missouri, impressed the two because it was here that free coffee came with good conversation at an antique store where they found old German music and books.

Matthias listed strong winds, especially in Texas and Arizona, as treacherous. The winds, along with the big trucks on the interstate, made for dangerous riding. The older sections of road were also hazardous in spots because of unexpected splits, bumps, and ridges. He recommends driving very cautiously in these sections.

Another problem they encountered is one all travelers find — a real lack of consistent Route 66 signage. He suggests investing in good trip guides, maps, and planning each day ahead. Matthias and Christina also picked up on American bad habits: we are wasteful and careless with roadside debris, including old cars and other junk. ■

HARLEY-DAVIDSON DUO-GLIDE

HARLEY-DAVIDSON "SPRINT"

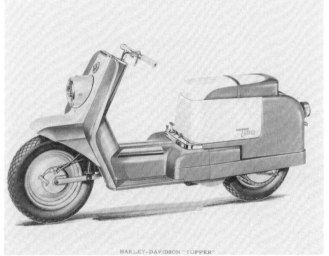

HARLEY-DAVIDSON "TOPPER"

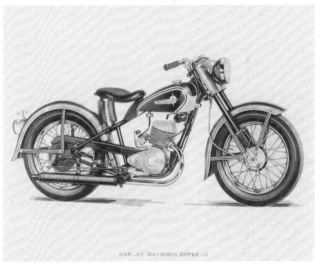

HARLEY-DAVIDSON SUPER-10

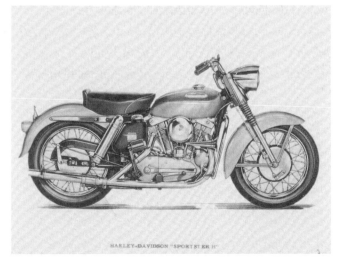

HARLEY-DAVIDSON "SPORTSTER H"

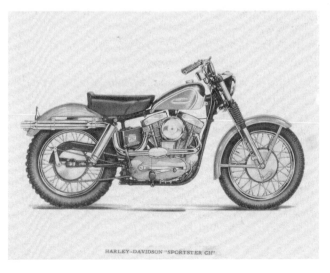

HARLEY-DAVIDSON "SPORTSTER CH"

1961 MOTORCYCLE LINE - HARLEY-DAVIDSON MOTOR CO.

Recipes from New Mexico

— MARIAN CLARK

Chorizo sausage came to America from Spain. The sausage is coarsely textured and very spicy. Widely used in Mexican cooking, it is suitable for slicing and can be found in many specialty shops in western Route 66 communities. A great recipe to begin or end a day of biking in this spectacular state.

Chorizo, Onion, and Potato Frittata

½ cup olive oil or vegetable oil
2 pounds russet potatoes, peeled and sliced in ¼ inch slices
2 onions, sliced in ¼-inch slices
8 ounces chorizo sausage
12 eggs
Salt and pepper to taste

Heat oil in a large heavy skillet. Add potatoes in batches and cook until tender and golden brown, about 8 minutes. Drain on paper towel.

Pour off all but 1 tablespoon of the oil. Add onions and sauté over medium low-heat until translucent. Increase heat and add sausages, crumbling with back of spoon. Cook for 5 minutes. Transfer onions and sausage to a large bowl. and add potatoes. Mix and toss together.

Preheat broiler. Beat eggs to blend. Pour over potato mixture. Season with salt and pepper. Spray a 12-inch broiler-proof skillet with nonstick spray. Pour egg-potato mixture into skillet. Reduce heat in broiler and cook frittata under broiler until eggs are set, about 10 minutes. Heat broiler again and broil fritta-

ta until top is lightly browned, about 3-4 minutes. Slide out onto plate and cut into wedges. Serve while hot with salsa, guacamole, sour cream, fresh tomatoes, and homemade toast. 8 servings.

Pecos Pueblo, Pecos National Historical Park

GRANOLA IS AWESOME BIKER FOOD. Here is the recipe served to guests at Alexander's Inn in Santa Fe. It packs well and makes for a great pick-me-up along the road.

Our Daily Granola
ALEXANDER'S INN

1 large (42-ounce) box old-fashioned oatmeal
½ cup wheat germ
½ cup oat bran

½ cup wheat bran
1 tablespoon cinnamon
1 cup each: walnuts, pecans, almonds
1 cup Canola oil
1 cup honey
1 cup maple syrup
1 cup molasses
3 tablespoons vanilla
2 teaspoons salt
1 cup each of coconut, chopped dates, dried cran-
    berries, and raisins (or other dried fruit to taste)

Preheat oven to 350 degrees. In a large roasting pan combine oatmeal, wheat germ, oat bran, wheat bran, cinnamon, and salt. Stir in chopped nuts. Combine oil, honey, syrup, molasses, and vanilla. Pour over mixture until all ingredients are coated. Bake for 30 minutes, stirring every ten minutes to cook evenly. Add dried fruit after removing from oven. This granola freezes well in airtight containers. Approximately 12 cups.

SOME OF THE BEST FOOD SERVED IN NEW MEXICO can be found at the bed and breakfast retreats hidden along the way. Hacienda Vargas Bed and Breakfast Inn, in Algodonas, is noted for good food amid pristine vistas. Frances Vargas shared these mouth-watering favorites, perfect for hungry appetites.

Chorizo Roll
HACIENDA VARGAS

4 links chorizo sausage
12 eggs
1½ cups milk

2 cups cheddar cheese
salt and pepper to taste
2 cups cubed French bread
8 ounces cream cheese
1 tablespoon diced green chili

Fry chorizo, chop into small pieces, and drain. Beat eggs and add all ingredients except cream cheese and green chili. Mix softened cream cheese with green chili and set aside. Spray non-stick cooking spray in a jelly roll pan. Line pan with foil, including sides. Spray foil generously with non-stick cooking spray.

Spread egg mixture into foil-lined pan. Bake for 45 minutes in preheated 350 degree oven until eggs are firm. Allow eggs to cool then turn pan out onto waxed paper; carefully peel off foil, using waxed paper to help. Spread cream cheese and green chili mixture over entire surface. Roll egg mixture to form a tight cylinder. Garnish with avocado and salsa recipe below. 6 servings.

Salsa
HACIENDA VARGAS

2 large tomatoes
½ cup tomato sauce
⅔ cup green chill roasted or 4 jalapeños peeled and chopped (Add chili to taste)
⅓ cup yellow onions
1 tablespoon fresh cilantro, finely chopped
2 teaspoons fresh parsley, finely chopped
2 teaspoons red wine vinegar
1 teaspoon freshly squeezed lemon juice
1 small hot dried red pepper, crushed

Combine all ingredients in a medium bowl, let salsa sit at room temperature for ½ hour then refrigerate. 3 cups.

It was almost a hundred years ago that pinto beans were first planted in the Estancia Valley. For many years the area was considered the pinto bean capital of the world.

Now Moriarty celebrates the heritage of beans at the Annual Pinto Bean Fiesta and Cook-off held the second Saturday each October. Why not schedule your trip to take part!

Stuffed Chiles
Moriarty Pinto Bean Fiesta

12 whole green chiles, roasted and peeled
1½ cups cooked pinto beans
½ cup Colby Jack cheese, shredded
1½ cups Swiss cheese, shredded
1 teaspoon garlic powder
Salt and pepper
4 eggs
Bread crumbs
Vegetable shortening for frying

Mash beans. Add cheeses, garlic powder, salt, and pepper and blend well. Make a small slice in each whole chile to enable stuffing. Place about 4 tablespoons of bean mixture in each chili.

Beat eggs until frothy. Dip chiles into egg and roll in bread crumbs. Pan fry until golden and cheese is melting. 6 servings.

Bizcochitos are the official State Cookie of New Mexico. Here is the recipe served at Bottger Mansion near Old Town.

Bizcochitos
(Official New Mexico State Cookie)

2 cups butter
1½ cups sugar
1 teaspoon anise seeds
2 eggs
6-7 cups sifted flour
1½ teaspoons baking powder
½ teaspoon salt
¼ cup milk (water, bourbon, or sherry may be substituted)
2 tablespoons sugar
1 teaspoon cinnamon

Cream butter, sugar, and anise seeds in a large mixing bowl. Add eggs and beat well.

Combine flour, baking powder, and salt in another mixing bowl. Add to creamed mixture along with milk or other liquid to form a stiff dough.

Knead dough slightly and pat or roll to a ¼-½ inch thickness. Cut dough into desired shapes with cookie cutter.

Combine sugar and cinnamon in a small bowl. Dust the top of each cookie with a small amount of the mixture.

Bake on greased cookie sheets in a preheated 400 degree oven for about 10 minutes or until cookies are slightly browned. 6 dozen, 2½ inch cookies.

Becky Steele of Albuquerque shared this easy casserole. Chilies relleños make for satisfying fare, especially when accompanied by green salad and fresh fruit. This is real comfort food, New Mexico style.

Chiles Relleños Casserole

6 eggs, separated
1 tablespoon flour
¼ teaspoon salt
¼ teaspoon pepper
1 4-ounce can whole green chilies
½ pound shredded cheddar cheese

Lightly spray an 8x11x2-inch baking pan with vegetable cooking spray. Beat egg whites until stiff. Combine flour, salt and pepper with egg yolks. Fold into whites and pour half of the mixture into baking pan. Slit chiles lengthwise and lay flat over egg mixture. Cover with grated cheese. Pour on remaining egg mixture. Bake in a preheated 325 degree oven for 25 minutes.
    4 servings.

Tortilla soup sells attitude — it's perfect for bikers. Adjust the seasoning to your own heat comfort level then kick back and enjoy!

Tortilla Soup

2 tablespoons corn oil
4 corn tortillas, cut in 1-inch strips
3 cloves garlic, minced
2 medium onions, chopped

Camillo Pinto visits the past, Barton

4 tomatoes, skinned and chopped
1 tablespoon ground cumin
½ to 1 jalapeño pepper (depending on heat desired)
8 cups chicken stock
¼ cup fresh cilantro
1 cup diced cooked chicken
Salt and pepper to taste

Garnishes:
Extra crisp fried strips of tortilla
Grated cheddar cheese
Diced avocado
Chopped cilantro

Heat oil in 4-quart stockpot and fry tortilla strips. Add garlic and onions and cook until onions are soft. Add remaining ingredients except chicken, bring to boil, then simmer in covered container for 20 minutes. Add chicken and continue simmering for 5 minutes more. Taste and add salt or pepper to taste.

Serve with garnishes in separate bowls. 8-10 generous servings.

When your New Mexico ride is over for the day, give in to a big platter of fajitas with your brothers and sisters from the road. Ron Chavez of the fabled Club Cafe in Santa Rosa referred to fajitas as "the new rage of the age." The same can be said for today's bike culture: Bikes are the rage of the age and riders are ready for rolling parties.

Sizzling Fajitas

¾ cup Italian dressing
1 (14 ounce) can green chilies, diced
1½ pounds of skirt or flank steak
1 large onion, sliced lengthwise
1 bell pepper
10 flour tortillas

Toppings:
Sliced avocado
Shredded Cheddar cheese
Sour cream
Jalapeño pepper slices

Combine dressing and chilies in 9x13-inch pan. Add meat, turning to coat with the mixture. Cover and refrigerate several hours or overnight, turning occasionally. Grill or broil meat, onions, and pepper to desired doneness. Slice meat across the grain, ½ inch thick.

Fill warm flour tortillas with meat, onion, pepper, and any toppings desired. Serve while hot.

10 servings.

THE 3RD ANNUAL INDIAN COUNTRY DINING GUIDE, published in Gallup, included enough recipes to satisfy every biker searching for authentic regional food — salsa, Navajo fry bread, enchilada casseroles, sopaipillas, green chili stew, piñon cookies, guacamole, chili con queso, gazpacho, and a wide variety of other native dishes. Here are some delicious examples.

Mary Muller's Posole Stew

1 pound lean pork shoulder
2 pounds frozen posole (hominy)
Juice of one lime
2 tablespoons coarse red chili
3 cloves garlic
¼ teaspoon dried oregano
Salt and pepper to taste

Cook the pork in a pressure cooker, with enough water to cover until tender. Reduce pressure under cold water. Open pot and add posole, lime juice and chili. Add water, about twice as much as the amount of posole. Cook under pressure again until done. Reduce pressure again under cold water. Remove the pork and cut it into small pieces. Return to cooker. Add oregano and salt. Continue to simmer without pressure for another 20 minutes or until hominy has burst but is not mushy. Serve as a main course or as a side dish.

Note: Adjust cooking time to your altitude, or see the instruction book for your pressure cooker. 8 servings.

Martha Joe's Navajo Fry Bread

3 cups flour (Use either white or half whole wheat flour.)
1½ teaspoons baking powder
½ teaspoon salt
1⅓ cups warm water
Shortening

Mix flour, baking powder, and salt. Add warm water to make a soft dough. Knead until smooth. Tear off a chunk of dough about the size of a small plum. Pat and stretch until it is thin. Poke a hole through the center and drop in sizzling hot deep fat (375 degrees). Lard is the traditional shortening, but vegetable oil is often used today. Brown on both sides. Drain and serve hot. Eat with honey or jam. 12-15 pieces.

Gazpacho New Mexico
"Liquid salad" from Spain with a special New Mexico touch.

2 pounds tomatoes
1 cucumber
1 large onion
½ green pepper
¼ cup olive oil
1 cup tomato juice
1 (4-ounce) can diced green chilies
2 large cloves garlic, minced
1 tablespoon vinegar
Salt and pepper to taste

Dice half the tomatoes, cucumber, onion, and green pepper. Set aside in large bowl. Combine the remaining half of the vegetables in a blender of food processor. Add the tomato juice, chilies, garlic, olive oil, and vinegar. Blend until smooth. Pour over container of chopped vegetables. Stir well and season to taste. Cover and chill thoroughly. Serve while very cold with garlic croutons or hot garlic bread. 8 servings.

THERE ARE SEVERAL VERSIONS of Mexican wedding cookies. After baking, there is a small hole in the center of each cookie. This is a recipe where substitutions don't work. Use real butter and cake flour, then pack some cookies along in your tank bag.

Mexican Wedding Cookies

2/3 cup pecans
1¾ cups powdered sugar
1 stick (8 tablespoons) butter, softened and cut
    into several pieces
¾ cup soft vegetable shortening
1 teaspoon vanilla
2½ cups cake flour
¼ teaspoon salt
Additional powdered sugar

Chop pecans and stir in a ½ cup of the powdered sugar. Set aside. Cream the butter and shortening until fluffy, then blend in vanilla.

Add remaining powdered sugar to the creamed mixture and beat until smooth. Add flour and salt, stirring just enough to combine. Stir in the nuts and sugar.

Form dough into ½-inch balls and place 1 inch apart on two lightly buttered cookie sheets. Bake in preheated 350 degree oven for 12 to 15 minutes. Cookies should not be browned. Cool on rack then sift a light coating of powdered sugar over cookies. 5½ dozen cookies.

THE FINAL SIXTEEN-MILE STRETCH of New Mexico Route 66 continues west on NM 118 into Manuelito. Stop to absorb the view and breathe deeply in this wide-open space. It's worth every minute. There is no ceiling over New Mexico and Arizona along here. The road skirts steep bluffs covered with the remnants of vintage advertisements, then crosses the border into Lupton. ■

End of an Era

— MICHAEL WALLIS

During the fifties, the bright neon lights began to dim along the Mother Road. It would be years before most people even noticed.

The seeds for the highway's demise were planted when the nation elected Dwight Eisenhower as president. During the war, the efficient German autobahn had impressed Eisenhower. He felt the United States could benefit from such highway technology and called for changes in the federal highway system. Proponents claimed that Route 66 was outdated and could no longer handle the increasing volume of traffic.

Ike's push for change was spelled out in 1956 guidelines for a new national interstate highway system.

Little by little over almost three decades the old road was replaced by a series of five interstate highways. The new roads cut off towns and cities and the familiar Route 66 shields were removed.

Finally, in 1984, the last of the Mother Road was bypassed at Williams, Arizona. There was a ceremony, speeches, and lots of news coverage. As the old highway's supporters pointed out, the opening of the new interstates made it possible to drive from Chicago all the way to the Pacific without stopping. And the government called that progress. ∎

133

Arizona

Fast facts from Arizona

- Approximate Route 66 mileage in Arizona — 376 miles

- In 1951, Winslow became the first Route 66 town in Arizona to establish one-way highway traffic, with 3rd Street westbound and 2nd Street eastbound.

- Winslow's "standing on the corner" sculpture is one of the most photographed spots in Arizona.

Standin' on the corner...

- Flagstaff's Museum Club has been ranked as one of the ten best roadhouses in America.

Arizona Biker Road Rules

- Safety Helmet, required by law under age 18

- Eye Protection, required by law unless equipped with windscreen

Must see in Arizona

- THE CONTINENTAL DIVIDE —
  - Try Highways 124 and 117 through the Indian reservations.
  - Visit with residents and soak up the atmosphere.

- HOLBROOK — Take US 180 southeast from Holbrook to ride through the Petrified Forest National Park.

- WINSLOW
  - See La Posada, the last Harvey House to be built along Route 66, now restored at 401 East Second Street.
  - Try South Mogollon Rim Drive for spectacular views! South on Highway 87 or 99
  - See the Meteor Crater 22 miles west off I-40

- FLAGSTAFF — Take Oak Creek Canyon – great biker drive south of town on Highway 89A for a spectacular 25 mile drive to visit the art center of Sedona.

- WILLIAMS — See Grand Canyon National Park, South Rim

- ASH FORK — Flagstone capital of the USA. Begin west of here to drive 178 miles of uninterrupted Route 66, all the way to Topock.

The Grand Canyon State

- *SELIGMAN* — Angel Delgadillo's Barber Shop and Visitor Center, 217 E. Route 66. Angel, a Steinbeck Award Winner, will make you feel welcome! This is a strongly recommended stop.

- *KINGMAN*
  - Powerhouse Visitors' Center, 120 West Andy Devine
  - Hualapai Mountain Park, a good ride, 12 miles southeast

- *PEACH SPRINGS* — See Burma Shave Style Signs recreated by American Safety Razor Company.

- *HACKBERRY* — Visit John and Kerry at the Old Route 66 Visitors Center, once owned by Bob Waldmire.

- *OATMAN*
  - Oatman Hotel where Clark Gable and Carol Lombard spent their wedding night
  - See "Panhandling" burros along the street, live gunfights on weekends and holidays and the "Jezebels Sashay" on weekend afternoons.
  - Watch bed races down Main Street in January, the International Burro Biscuit Toss each September, and the Sidewalk Egg Fry Competition each Fourth of July.

Where to buy stuff in Arizona

- *JOSEPH CITY* — Jack Rabbit Trading Post

- *WINSLOW* — Roadworks Gifts & Souvenirs

- *SELIGMAN* — Angel Delgadillo's Visitor Center and Gift Shop

Beacons in the dark

- HOLBROOK — Wigwam Village Motel. Elinor Lewis, manager, is daughter of Chester Lewis who built the motel in 1950.

Wigwam Village Motel, Holbrook

- WILLIAMS
  - THE RED GARTER BED AND BAKERY, 137 W. Railroad Avenue, (520) 635-1484 or 1 800-328-1484
  - CANYON COUNTRY INN, 442 W. Bill Williams Ave., (520) 635-2349 or 1 800 643-1020

- KINGMAN — Hotel Brunswick, 315 East Andy Devine

Favorite hangouts for food and drink

- HOLBROOK
  - JOE AND AGGIE'S, 120 West Hopi Drive. A must stop, the oldest restaurant in Holbrook still in business
  - BUTTERFIELD STAGE COMPANY, 609 W. Hopi Drive

- WINSLOW
  - FALCON RESTAURANT, 1113 East 3rd
  - SANTA FE WHISTLE STOP, 114 East 3rd Street A Valentine diner on the site of the first house in Winslow

- FLAGSTAFF
  - MUSEUM CLUB, 3404 East Route 66. Depression era roadhouse. Highly recommended
  - MIZ ZIP'S, since the 1950s, 2924 East Route 66
  - BEAVER STREET BREWERY & WHISTLE STOP CAFE, 11 South Beaver Street

- WILLIAMS
  - ROD'S STEAK HOUSE, 301 East Bill Williams
  - TWISTERS, a 50's Soda Fountain, 417 East Route 66

- SELIGMAN
  - DELGADILLO'S SNOW CAP, on Historic Route 66
  - COPPER CART RESTAURANT, on Historic Route 66

- KINGMAN —
  - MR. D'S, 105 Andy Devine
  - CITY CAFE, 1929 East Andy Devine
  - VICTORIA'S MEMORY LANE, 120 West Andy Devine

- TRUXTON — Frontier Cafe. Mildred Barker operates the cafe and motel and has a great story about how the cafe originated.

- OATMAN — Oatman Hotel Raggedy Ass Miners Bar

The Museum Club, Flagstaff

Three Piece

— MICHAEL WALLIS

Paul loves his Harley more than anything else on earth. He spends so much time in the saddle riding America's highways that his legs are beginning to bow, just like a cowboy's.

After sweating on the assembly line for Ford Motor Company in Detroit ever since he was a kid, Paul said the hell with it. He retired, drew his last pay, and some pretty decent benefits to boot. Then he jumped on his bike. He's been out on the open road ever since.

Paul cruises any and all two-lanes but one of his favorites is Route 66. He's ridden the Mother Road all the way from Chicago to Santa Monica and tries to fit in a stretch of the old highway every chance he gets.

One summer evening at Flagstaff — a Route 66 town that serves as the unofficial capital of northern Arizona — Paul was motoring his trusty Harley back to a motel room after a night spent two-stepping at a lively street party. Paul felt no pain — not from booze or weed but from hours of sucking down thin air as he boogied to the sounds of a turned-on rock n' roll outfit.

Just as he made an easy turn onto Route 66, Paul — his windpipes and head clogged from ripe sagebrush and cottonwood — cut loose with a great sneeze. Much to his dismay Paul not only cleared out his sinuses but his upper false teeth plate went flying into time and space. He watched in disbelief as his airborne choppers disappeared into the night.

In a flash, Paul manufactured a U-turn, parked his bike, and broke out his Zippo. The cigarette lighter wasn't nearly bright enough to do him much good and

after a half-hour of searching the weeds and brush, Paul gave up. He got on his bike and headed for the barn.

Three Piece (far right) celebrates with fellow bikers, Flagstaff

Next morning, his stomach growling for breakfast, Paul slugged down some hot Joe and headed back to the spot on the Mother Road where he and his top teeth parted ways. No sooner had Paul begun his daylight search when one of Flagstaff's finest pulled up. The curious lady officer asked Paul what he was up to and when he told her his pitiful yarn she doubled up in laughter. Once she regained her composure, the cop pitched right in and helped Paul scour the high grasses.

A little later, she called for some backup and before too long, a couple more squad cars arrived on the scene. The cluster of police vehicles and lone Harley attracted the attention of some other passing bikers and soon the search party had expanded to ten strong.

Together the cops and bikers systematically searched the ditches and poked through the weeds. Finally one of the officers shouted, "I found 'em!" Everyone turned to see the cop holding aloft Paul's upper plate — in three separate pieces. Although the teeth were less than whole the search party cheered in unison.

After thanking everyone and shaking hands all around, Paul leaped on his Harley and rode straight to the Wal-Mart store. He bought a tube of Super Glue and headed to the store men's room where he carefully put his teeth back together. He tucked them in his pocket to let the glue dry and by the end of the afternoon the dentures were back in place.

Paul, delighted that he wouldn't have to gum down his meals, celebrated with a steak dinner. When his pals toasted him, he flashed his trademark smile and boasted: "Some might get their kicks on this road but I found my grin on Route 66!"

From that day on, Paul, the grinning biker from Detroit City, became known as "Three Piece." The name has stuck, just like that glue that still binds his teeth. Keep an eye out for him on the open road. He is still out there. You'll know him when you see him. Look for that wide smile and those pearly whites. ∎

Easy Rider

— MICHAEL WALLIS

Sweet Suzanne and I were riding our trusty Harley — with yellow Route 66 shields painted on the gas tank — along that old piece of Mother Road at Bellemont, Arizona. We were intent on visiting a true piece of pop culture history — the Pine Breeze Inn.

This was the establishment made famous in "Easy Rider," the classic biker film from 1969, starring Dennis Hopper as "Billy the Kid" and Peter Fonda as "Captain America." As children of the turbulent 60s, we are fans of the film that helped define that time and capture the true feelings of disenfranchised American youths.

The Pine Breeze Inn, about a dozen miles west of Flagstaff, is one of several sites along Route 66 that appeared in the movie. Since we were in the neighborhood, Suzanne and I thought it only appropriate to pay our respects. We remembered the scene very well — Hopper and Fonda pull their choppers up to the inn with its neon "Vacancy" sign glowing out front. Then the proprietor cracks open the door, takes one look at the pair outside, and flips on "No" in front of "Vacancy." The stunned bikers angrily ride off down Route 66 and camp in the forest.

Michael Wallis at the Pine Breeze Inn

When we pulled up to the Pine Breeze, it was clear things had changed. We could still make out the words, "Pine Breeze Inn" and "All Credit Cards Accepted" in the fading paint but the place was boarded up and deserted.

Another biker was already there snooping around. He stood in front of the building and it appeared he was writing something on the wall. Then he walked back to his bike, nodded a silent greeting to us, and left. Suzanne took some photos and we walked all around the property not really knowing what we were hunting for, unless it was some of our own memories from the past.

I approached the Pine Breeze and thought I would see what kind of graffiti our fellow biker had left behind. Maybe he wrote his name and the date or else tattooed the wall with some clever biker saying. He had done neither. I found only "66 Lives" penciled on the wall. That was all. That was enough.

We left the Pine Breeze and went just a short distance down the old road to grab some lunch at the nearby Route 66 Roadhouse Bar and Grill, next to the busy Harley shop. The Roadhouse was a biker's nirvana. Not only was it brimming with riders from all across the land, but also there was plenty of biker memorabilia, including a World War II Harley. Of course, the irony of the scene did not escape us since we found ourselves so close to a site once identified with anti-biker sentiments.

Then as we scanned the crowd for familiar faces while eating our lunch we both happened to looked up about the same time. There hanging from the ceiling in all its glory was the "No Vacancy" sign from "Easy Rider." We had come full circle. The tale was complete. We raised our burgers in a triumphant toast to the old sign and to Captain America and Billy and to a time when we were all nature's true children. ∎

The Pine Breeze

Recipes from Arizona
— MARIAN CLARK

The Holbrook Summer Indian Dance Program includes a recipe for Navajo tacos, shared by the Holbrook Chamber of Commerce. Rather than using Mexican-style tortillas, Navajo fry bread forms the base for this popular fare. Every biker must try these!

Navajo Tacos

To make Fry Bread:
4 cups white flour
8 teaspoons baking powder
1 cup powdered milk
1 teaspoon salt (optional)
Warm water as needed

Mix flour, baking powder, powdered milk, and salt. Slowly add warm water to mixture to make a medium-stiff dough, soft enough to easily shape, but not sticky. Hand knead to form a ball about 4 inches in diameter. Shape into 4 flat discs about 8 inches in diameter. The dough should be about ¼ inch thick. Use of a rolling pin is not recommended. Add a small amount of flour if the dough becomes too sticky to handle.

Deep fry in hot oil (375 degrees). When a large bubble forms, pop it with a fork. When the sides begin to brown, turn and finish frying on other side.

Serve while hot, topped with pinto beans, ground beef or other diced meat, diced lettuce, tomato, onion, and grated cheese. Add other toppings like guacamole, sour cream, or hot salsa, if desired. 4 servings.

THIS PIZZA MAKES A DELICIOUS CASUAL MEAL that is unusual because of the tortilla crust topped with a delicious combination of seasoned beef and chopped vegetables.

Holbrook Mexican Pizza

6 ounces ground beef
½ package (1.25-ounces) taco seasoning mix
2 flour tortillas (10-inch size)
1 cup grated cheddar cheese
1 cup chopped tomatoes, drained
⅓ cup sliced green onion
¼ cup diced black olives

Two Guns, Arizona

2 tablespoons minced green pepper
1½ tablespoons sliced pickled jalapeño chilies, drained
1 cup grated Monterey Jack cheese

Cook beef and taco seasoning in heavy skillet until brown, crumbling with fork until separated. Remove and cool.

In same skillet, add a tortilla and cook until crisp, about 2 minutes, turning once. Remove and cook second tortilla until crisp. Leave this tortilla in skillet and reduce heat to low. Sprinkle Cheddar cheese over tortilla. Top with second tortilla. Heat until cheese melts, pressing with a spatula, about 2 minutes. Preheat broiler. Transfer tortillas to a pizza pan. Top with cooked beef, sprinkle with tomato, onion, olives,

green pepper, and chiles. Top with Monterey Jack cheese. Broil until cheese melts, about 3 minutes. Cut into wedges and serve.

2 servings, or 6 appetizers.

ED WOJCIAK WANDERED WEST FROM NEW JERSEY in 1976 when Flagstaff had only about fifty restaurants. He and his wife, Brandy, soon opened La Bellavia in the old downtown section of the city where a pizza parlor, Chicken Delight, and sub shop had once served nearby college students. La Bellavia remains a comfortable place that serves quality food, a favorite of local residents, and a great biker stop for breakfast or lunch.

Zucchini Quiche
La Bellavia

12 ounces of fresh zucchini, grated
1 small onion, diced
1 tablespoon cooking oil
10 ounces Swiss cheese, grated
7 eggs
2 cups milk
Salt and pepper to taste
1 baked 10-inch crust
¼ teaspoon nutmeg

Sauté grated zucchini and onion in cooking oil until onion is golden. Meanwhile, whip the eggs and add milk, salt and pepper to taste. Add the cheese and the zucchini mixture to the eggs. Pour into a baked 10-inch pie pan and sprinkle lightly with nutmeg. Place pie pan on a cookie sheet and bake the quiche in a preheated 350 degree oven for 1 hour. Allow to stand 5-10 minutes before slicing. 6 large or 8 medium servings.

WHEN I INQUIRED ABOUT GOOD COOKS IN THE FLAGSTAFF AREA, the first person mentioned was Roabie Johnson, who works at the Flagstaff Library. Roabie grew up in Albuquerque and moved to Flagstaff to attend college. She loves the outdoors and worked for several years as a river guide. This potato recipe was a great favorite on trips. Even though it is a large recipe and is given with outdoor directions, it can be easily adapted for the oven and is certainly a biker favorite.

Roabie Johnson's Wild and Scenic Dutch-Oven Cowboy Spuds

1 pound bacon, chopped
5 pounds potatoes, washed and cut in large chunks
2 onions, each sliced in 6-8 pieces
3 cans beer
2 packages onion soup mix (1.15 ounces each)
1 pound Longhorn or Jack cheese, grated

Fry the bacon in a Dutch oven until brown. Pour off most of the grease. Add potatoes, onions, beer, and soup mix. Cook over the fire, on a grill, or on the ground with coals on the top and bottom of the Dutch oven. Add more coals to the top if the oven cools too much. You should be able to hold hands comfortably about 10 inches above the Dutch oven lid. Stir occasionally. Add more beer if needed. The potatoes should cook in about 1½ hours. When the liquid is thick and the potatoes are done, place cheese on top. Heat until melted.

The potatoes are good for breakfast with eggs, if there are any leftovers. Bake these potatoes in your oven at home when you aren't cooking outdoors. 15-20 servings.

Roabie Johnson says her mother is a wonderful Southern cook who blended her culinary roots with her western environment. This bread recipe is an adaptation from her mother.

Roabie Johnson's Heirloom Bread

3 cups white flour
1 cup whole wheat flour
2 teaspoons baking powder
1½ teaspoons baking soda

½ teaspoon salt

2 teaspoons cinnamon

½ teaspoon nutmeg

½ teaspoon ground clove

1½ cups sugar

1 cup margarine

4 eggs

2 teaspoons vanilla

2 cups applesauce

2 cups chopped pecans

1 cup currants

Combine dry ingredients; set aside. Cream margarine and sugar. Add eggs, vanilla, and applesauce. Add to dry mixture and blend until smooth. Stir in pecans and currants. Grease 2 9x5x3-inch loaf pans. Bake in preheated 350 degree oven for 1 hour or until bread tests done with a toothpick inserted into the center. 2 loaves.

"Cruisin'" Susan Daly at the Old Route 66 Visitors Center, Hackberry

LONGTIME FLAGSTAFF RESIDENT, PEGGY HARRIS, was born near Springfield, Missouri, another Route 66 community. She said she never wanted to be a dull ho-hum-type cook, so she does a lot of experimenting. Peggy says her friends go nuts over her mulligatawny soup. For years she didn't have a recipe, but prepared it by using a pinch of this and that. Finally, they insisted she write out some directions. Peggy says this soup is one that requires tasting to adjust flavors for individual preferences. But what hearty, comfortable results! Perfect after a long day on the bike.

Peggy Harris' Mulligatawny Soup

1 onion

1 large or 2 small carrots

3 stalks celery

4 tablespoons flour

4 tablespoons butter or margarine

4 cups chicken stock

2 cups chopped cooked chicken

2 tart cooking apples, chopped

2 cups cooked rice

2 teaspoons curry powder

1 teaspoon (approximately) of each of the following:
    turmeric

cardamom, coriander, garlic, and salt.

½ teaspoon pepper

2 cups cream

Chop onion, carrots and celery finely by hand or in the food processor. Melt the butter or margarine and saute vegetables in heavy skillet until tender. Add enough flour to make a roux. More margarine may be necessary.

In a stock pot, heat the chicken stock and chicken. Add the apples and rice. Stir in the vegetables and seasonings, adjusting quantity to your individual taste. Stir in the cream just before serving. Approximately 10 cups.

Christina Hey at the Grand Canyon

BEAVER STREET BREWERY AND WHISTLE STOP CAFE can be found on the corner of Phoenix and Beaver Streets, just south of the railroad tracks and historic downtown Flagstaff. The original building was constructed in 1938 of Malapais rock collected from surrounding volcanic beds.

Beaver Street Brewery and Whistle Stop Cafe opened in March of 1994, featuring handcrafted brews by owner and brewmaster Evan Hanseth. It is a great biker stop.

This rib-sticking chili is a favorite that is bound to satisfy!

Easy Ridin' in Bellemont

Grand Canyon Harley-Davidson/Buell can be found in Bellemont, Arizona, a tiny hamlet west of Flagstaff that caters to bikers. The town's fame is due in part to the Pine Breeze Inn, made famous when Easy Rider characters, Captain America and Billy, failed to find a room on their fateful 1969 biker cruise. The inn remains boarded up today, but bikers are now welcome to camp on the 2½-acre property. Just down the road, both the highly successful Grand Canyon Harley-Davidson facility and the Route 66 Roadhouse Bar and Grill, pay tribute to everything Harley.

At the roadhouse, the "No Vacancy" sign from the movie hangs from the ceiling. Table tops are glass-covered motorcycle wheels, a World War II cycle stands next to a "Harley Parking Only" sign, and a Harley-Davidson juke box cranks out road music in one corner.

Felix and Lori Mansane built the roadhouse and frequently use it for biker parties and charity events. Mansane has been an avid biker for over forty years.

One of the few other establishments in Bellemont is a bar named Junior's, where more bikers gather. Bellemont residents agree that biking today is about the ride and recreation. They appreciate Harley bikers who are most often middle-aged businessmen and women who have the money to express the Harley distinction. Bellemont is a biker "must stop."

Hart Prairie Chili

BEAVER STREET BREWERY AND WHISTLE STOP CAFE

Brown together in a large skillet:
2 tablespoons canola oil
2½ pounds of beef chuck roast, trimmed and cut
    into ¼ inch cubes
1½ pounds of beef chuck roast, trimmed and
coarsely ground
1 red bell pepper, diced in ½-inch pieces
1 fresh poblano chili, diced in ½-inch pieces
1 red onion, cut in strips
1 tablespoon fresh garlic, minced

When vegetables become translucent, add:
½ cup chili powder
2 tablespoons cumin
1 tablespoon garlic powder
1 tablespoon onion powder
1 teaspoon cayenne pepper
1 tablespoon kosher salt
1 tablespoon oregano

And finally, add:
1 cup bitter ale or other mild beer
4 cups chicken broth
4 cups diced canned tomatoes in juice
Simmer for 20 minutes then add:
2 cups black beans, cooked and drained
2 cups kidney beans, cooked and drained
2 cups pinto beans, cooked and drained

Continue simmering until meat is tender and chili
is hot.

Serve immediately to a large crowd, or cover
tightly and store in refrigerator briefly, or freeze.
20 servings.

FOOD FOR GRAZING, PREFERABLY WITH THE FINGERS, is
always popular around Bellemont. This recipe is typical
of the easy yet good fare that is just as popular with the
guys as with the gals.

Hot Artichoke Dip

½ cup chopped onion
1 teaspoon butter
1 can (14 ounces) artichoke hearts, chopped in ½
    inch pieces
1 cup low-fat mayonnaise
1 cup grated Parmesan cheese
⅓ cup picante sauce (mild or hot, depending on
taste)
Garlic salt to taste

Saute the onion in butter. Combine with remaining
ingredients and pour into a shallow 8-inch casserole
dish. Bake in a preheated 350 degree oven for 15 to
20 minutes or until bubbly and light brown. Serve
warm with crackers or toast squares. Approximately
10 servings.

LOCATED ON WHISKEY ROW IN DOWNTOWN WILLIAMS, *The
Red Garter Bed and Bakery* is housed in a fully restored
1897 bordello. John Holst, the innkeeper, carefully reno-
vated the historic building at 137 Railroad Avenue. He
opened *The Red Garter Bed and Bakery* in 1994. There is
a honeymoon suite, the madam's room at the top of the
stairs, and two rooms formerly called cribs. A full-service bakery and coffee shop is located in the downstairs
turn-of-the-century saloon. Holst has many historic
photographs and a wealth of stories to share.

Gingerbran Muffins
RED GARTER BED AND BAKERY

½ cup oil
⅔ cup molasses
2 eggs
¼ cup milk
2 cups flour
1½ teaspoons baking powder
1 teaspoon ground ginger
½ teaspoon cinnamon
½ teaspoon nutmeg
¼ teaspoon ground cloves
¼ cup wheat bran

Grease 8-10 2-inch muffin tins. Combine oil, molasses, eggs, and milk. Mix well. Stir flour with baking soda and spices. Add to liquid mixture but do not over-mix. Pour muffin batter into tins. Sprinkle tops with wheat bran. Bake in preheated 350 degree oven for 20 minutes or until browned. 8-10 muffins

El Tovar Chili
GRAND CANYON NATIONAL PARK LODGES

1½ pound diced filet mignon
1 pound diced pork loin
1 white onion, diced fine
1 jalapeño pepper, chopped fine
1 tablespoon fresh garlic

Linda Scott watches train from bridge at Correro

3 (12-ounce) cans beer
3 tablespoons chili powder
1 tablespoon paprika
1 tablespoon cumin
1 tablespoon Tabasco sauce
½ cup diced tomatoes
½ cup tomato sauce
Salt and pepper to taste
½ cup grated Monterey Jack cheese

Sauté the filet mignon, pork loin, onion, and jalapeño pepper.

Add remaining ingredients. Add salt and pepper and simmer for 2-3 hours on low heat.

To serve, put a serving of chili into oven-proof bowl, top with Jack cheese, and put under broiler for a few moments until cheese is melted and slightly brown. Serve with blue corn chips and a slab of cornbread. 6 portions.

ANGEL DELGADILLO IS THE DRIVING FORCE behind the Historic Route 66 Association of Arizona and is loved by Route 66 travelers from coast to coast. He operates his barber shop just a few doors from his late brother Juan Delgadillo's Snow Cap in Seligman. Both establishments are "must see" stops for Route 66 bikers.

Trond and his band from Norway make this a regular stop and bikers from around the world join them. German biker, Matthias Guenther, stopped for a haircut, gifts, and small talk with Angel and recommended staying at the Aztec Motel across the street from Angel's shop.

Angel is interviewed regularly for specials about Route 66 that are shown around the world. Stop, too, at the grocery store next to the barber shop. Juan and Angel's brother, Joe, operated it until his retirement. It's a friendly place with a good deli.

Angel's wife Vilma shares these favorite family recipes.

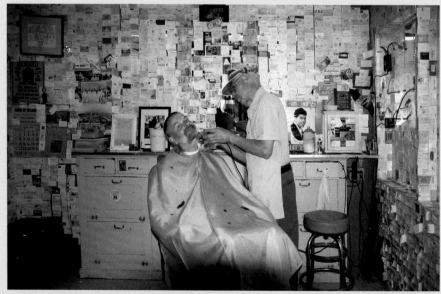

A trip highlight, Angel Delgadillo trims Matthias Guenther's beard in his famous Seligman barber shop

Martha Delgadillo's Impossible Quesa-dillo Pie

2 (4-ounce) cans chopped green chilies
4 cups shredded cheese (about 1 pound)
2 cups milk
1 cup baking mix (Bisquick)
4 eggs

Preheat oven to 425 degrees. Grease a 10-inch pie plate. Sprinkle chilies and cheese in plate. Blend milk, baking mix and eggs until smooth in a blender, food processor, or with a hand beater for at least a minute. Pour mixture into pie plate. Bake 25-30 minutes or until knife inserted in the center comes out clean. Let stand 10 minutes before cutting. 8 slices.

Aztec Motel, Seligman

Vilma Delgadillo's Chiles Relleños Casserole

1 pound ground beef
½ cup chopped onion
½ teaspoon salt
¼ teaspoon pepper
2 (4-ounce) cans green chiles, peeled, cut in halves
    lengthwise and seeded

Several dashes hot sauce
1½ cups shredded longhorn cheese
1½ cups milk
¼ cup flour
½ teaspoon salt
Dash of pepper
4 eggs

In a skillet, brown beef and onions. Drain fat. Sprinkle meat with salt and pepper. Spread half the chiles in a 10x6-inch baking dish. Sprinkle with cheese and top with meat mixture. Arrange remaining chiles over meat. Beat egg whites until foamy. Combine egg yolks with milk, flour, salt and pepper. Fold into whites and pour over meat. Bake in a preheated 350 degree oven until knife comes out clean when inserted in center, about 30 minutes. 6 servings.

Angel and Vilma Delgadillos' Route 66 Gift Shop, Seligman

Juan Delgadillo's Snow Cap is run by his family since Juan's death in 2004.

HAVE COFFEE AND DESSERT WITH MILDRED BARKER at the Frontier Cafe in Truxton. Mildred tells a great story about the original owner, Alice Wright. It seems Alice inherited some money in Los Angeles. Alice believed in the occult, so when a fortune teller told her to travel 400 miles from Los Angeles and build a cafe, she did just that. When she arrived in Truxton, she had traveled the 400 miles, so she built her cafe and settled in.

Old-Fashioned Banana Pudding
FRONTIER CAFE

2½ cups evaporated milk
4 eggs, separated
⅔ cup sugar
6 tablespoons cornstarch
1 tablespoon butter
½ teaspoon vanilla
Pinch of salt
Vanilla wafer cookies
2-3 bananas

Scald the milk and stir in beaten egg yolks. Combine sugar and corn starch, stir into egg mixture. Add butter and continue stirring until mixture has thickened. Add vanilla and pinch of salt.

Line a 2-quart dish with cookies. Slice bananas over the cookies. Pour pudding mixture over bananas and allow to cool. If desired, whip egg whites and add ½ cup sugar. Spread over pudding and place in preheated 400 degree oven for 5 minutes to brown. 8 servings.

JACKIE ROWLAND IS A TRANSPLANTED OKIE who runs Fast Fanny's Place in Oatman. She has watched this tiny forgotten mining town come to life again, because tourists have rediscovered mountain life above those hairpin turns that were once necessary in order to proceed along Route 66.

Here is Jackie's favorite breakfast recipe, quick to prepare and always satisfying. She keeps tortillas and chorizo in the freezer so she can prepare the dish for "roadies" who often drop by for a visit. Add a couple more eggs and another tortilla or two to stretch the recipe when more folks show up than expected.

The salsa recipe is a prize winner, first served at one of the local chili cook-off competitions.

Jackie's Mexi Breakfast

FAST FANNY'S PLACE

½ pound beef or pork chorizo (Mexican sausage)
12-14 corn tortillas
4 tablespoons margarine
6-8 eggs, beaten

1 cup diced tomatoes, drained
1 medium bell pepper, diced
1 small onion, diced
1 cup shredded cheddar cheese

Garnishes:
Sour cream
Guacamole
Warm salsa

In a large skillet brown the chorizo, then remove. Add margarine and the tortillas torn in 1-inch pieces. Warm to soften. Add chorizo to egg mixture and fold in diced vegetables. Pour over tortillas and cook in skillet, stirring occasionally until eggs are set. Sprinkle with cheese then cover skillet until cheese is melted.

Serve with garnishes of sour cream, guacamole and salsa. 4 servings.

Linda Ellithorpe's Jailhouse Salsa

2 cans (15½ ounces each) tomatoes, mashed
1 can (8 ounces) tomato sauce
1 cup minced onion
1 cup minced bell pepper
2 cans (4.5 ounces each) chopped mild chilies
Garlic powder, oregano, cilantro, salt and pepper to taste

Mix well and serve over Mexi Breakfast or with tortilla chips. 6 cups.

"UNCLE CHARLIE HICKS" IS ANOTHER OKIE who has retired to Oatman. Uncle Charlie bartends at the Oatman Hotel, is the head gunfighter with the Ghostrider Gunfighters every weekend, and as "Reverend Uncle Charlie Hicks," is the local marrying and burying preacher.

Uncle Charlie collected this stew recipe while doing a stint as a gold prospector. Be sure to look him up when in Oatman.

Uncle Charlie Hicks' Beer Stew with Drop Dumplings

Beer Stew:
2 pounds lean beef, cut into chunks
1 large onion, coarsely chopped
1 (15½ ounce) can beef broth
1 can beer
1 bay leaf
3 tablespoons brown sugar
¼ cup red wine vinegar

Brown beef and onions together in a large stew pot. Add broth, beer, bay leaf, sugar, and vinegar. Cover and simmer until meat is tender.

Drop Dumplings:
1 cup flour
1 teaspoon salt
½ teaspoon baking soda
Milk to make a stiff, sticky batter

Mix dry ingredients. Add milk slowly. Drop by spoonfuls into bubbling stew. A little water may be needed. Cover and steam for twenty minutes. 6 servings.

Oatman Hotel

TAKE THAT WINDING HILL from Oatman to Golden Shores in the daylight as you head to the Colorado River and California! ■

Beacons in the Darkest Hours

— MICHAEL WALLIS

The Mother Road never really disappeared. Those of us who love history and popular culture knew that would not happen. The shields were taken down and whole towns cut off, but the spirit and legend of the highway could not be destroyed. Neither could the people.

Mother Road veterans — Ted Drewes, Lillian Redman, Angel Delgadillo, and others — could not be stopped from fanning to life that spark of pure energy that remained. They heard the poetry of the road and answered the call. They switched on their bright signs. Images of blue swallows, bucking horses, and Indian chiefs lured folks back to the road America loved best. The blue swallows took flight. The magic still worked.

Neon ribbons popped back to life and, like beacons, showed the way. Clusters of flickering light tempted interstate travelers like ribbons of sweet candy.

Route 66 came alive each time a neon sign was ignited, or someone hummed Bobby Troup's highway anthem, or read about the Joads, or watched a rerun of the television series, or rode through time and space on one of the old alignments.

It comes to life every time a biker heads into the wind on the old two-lane.

Like a revived neon marquee, the highway found new life. The Mother Road remains stronger than ever. ■

California

Fast facts from California

- There are approximately 312 miles of Route 66 in California.

- The state is our nation's third largest in area, but first in population.

- More than 300,000 tons of grapes are grown here annually and more than 17 million gallons of wine are made each year in the state.

- San Bernardino County is the largest in the nation with nearly three million acres.

California Biker Road Rules

- Safety Helmet, required by law

- Eye Protection, no restriction

Must see in California

- NEEDLES
  - El Garces — A former Harvey House and depot
  - Enjoy side trips to Laughlin and Havasu City.
  - East Mojave National Scenic Area and Goffs Schoolhouse. Tours begin at Essex Road.
- AMBOY — Roy's Cafe and Motel — recently under new ownership

- BARSTOW
  - Casa Del Desierto, a former Harvey Hotel, now the train and bus depot
  - Side trip to Calico Ghost Town, 11 miles northeast on I-15

Bikers at trail's end, Santa Monica

The Golden State

- *HELENDALE*
  - Dixie Lee Evans' Exotic World Burlesque Museum
  - Miles Mahan's Bottle Tree Museum

- *VICTORVILLE* — California Route 66 Museum

- *FONTANA* — Old Route 66 Orange Juice stand next to newly reopened Bono's Burgers

- *AZUZA* — The San Gabriel Canyon Road offers a great biker ride.

- *MONROVIA* — Aztec Hotel, 311 West Foothill Blvd. The only example of Mayan architecture along Route 66

- *PASADENA* — Rose Bowl Parade on New Year's Day (on old Route 66)

- *SANTA MONICA*
  - Santa Monica Pier — An antique carrousel, and ocean excitement
  - Will Rogers State Historic Park, 1501 Will Rogers State Park Road, Pacific Palisades Drive

★ **Sacramento**

⊙ **San Francisco**

CALIFORNIA

⊙ **San Bernardino**

⊙ **Los Angeles**

Ocean Ave., Santa Monica

155

Favorite hangouts for food and drink

- NEEDLES
  - 66 Burger Hut, 701 West Broadway
  - Hungry Bear, 1906 Needles Highway

- LUDLOW — Ludlow Cafe

- NEWBERRY SPRINGS — Bagdad Cafe (aka Sidewinder Cafe), 46548 National Trails Highway

- BARSTOW — Idle Spurs Steakhouse, 690 Hwy 58

- VICTORVILLE
  - La Fonda Mexican Restaurant, 15556 6th Street. Good food near the Route 66 Museum
  - Emma Jean's Hollandburger Cafe, 17143 D Street, on Route 66

- CAJON PASS — Summit Inn — on Route 66 since 1952. Off I-15, Cajon Pass, Oak Hill Road Exit

- SAN BERNARDINO — Mitla Cafe, 602 North Mt. Vernon. A longtime Mexican favorite on old Route 66

- RANCHO CUCAMONGA — Magic Lamp, 8189 Foothill Blvd.

- UPLAND — Buffalo Inn, 1814 West Foothill Blvd. A favorite for students from nearby Claremont. Try the "buffalo chips" with your burgers.

- MONROVIA — The Brass Elephant, 311 West Foothill Blvd., inside the Aztec Hotel

- Pasadena — Fair Oaks Pharmacy, corner of Mission and Fair Oaks

- WEST HOLLYWOOD
  - Barney's Beanery, 8447 Santa Monica Blvd.
  - Formosa Cafe, 7156 Santa Monica Blvd.

- SANTA MONICA
  - Rusty's Surf Ranch, 256 Santa Monica Pier
  - Ye Old King's Head British Pub, 116 Santa Monica Blvd.

Posse of road-weary bikers above the Pacific, Santa Monica

Bagdad Cafe

—MICHAEL WALLIS

A band of bikers, almost two weeks on the road, were nearing the tail end of a ride down the entire length of Route 66. It was July in high desert country where the temperature soars, so the bikers — in an effort to outfox the merciless sun — pulled out of Kingman in the dark wee hours. California bound, they wound their way up the twisty two-lane to funky Oatman tucked away in the Black Mountains. Everyone dropped into second gear in the old mining town where the populace and the wandering burros that tourists take pleasure in feeding still slumbered beneath the moonglow.

The riders followed the old Mother Road out of Oatman. The path, flanked with yucca, mesquite, and greasewood, leads to the land of milk and honey that lured hordes of Okies and Dust Bowl pilgrims during the tough lean years of the 1930s.

Daylight was still a rumor when the Harleys buzzed across the Colorado River and entered California near the venerable Route 66 town of Needles. After pancakes and pots of coffee at the Hungry Bear Restaurant the bikers topped off their gas tanks, checked tire pressures, and tied "cowboy air conditioners" — bandanas soaked in ice water — around their necks.

The great Mojave Desert awaited. So did a string of sunburned towns and ghost places along Route 66 making its way westward to Barstow before it cuts down to San Bernardino and turns toward Los Angeles, finally reaching Santa Monica on the Pacific. The cool ocean breezes seemed a lifetime away. That did not matter. The bikers figured to make it as far as Barstow in time to get rooms and cool off in a swimming pool before supper. There was no hurry; no one was in a rush.

All of them actually had looked forward to this leg of the trip. They realized the Mojave is special because it has a little bit of everything, especially the unex-

Mojave Desert

pected. The climate can be extreme, ranging from bitter cold in the winter to the summer when the temperature regularly reaches well into triple digits. Lying in the rain-shadow of the coastal mountain ranges, the Mojave receives average annual precipitation of less than six inches. Dry winds bring cloudless days, which means barely any rain. Plants, animals, and people learn to adapt or perish.

Yet sometimes from July to September, heavy and even violent rainstorms erupt as if from nowhere. On this particular day there was hardly a breeze and new-born clouds were forming. The bikers kept watch on the open skies all around them as they moved between inter-state highway and old road alignments through the remains of Goffs, where they inspected a restored schoolhouse. From there they continued on to Essex and then ahead to take photos and slug down bottled water at the remains of Danby, Summit, and Chambless.

Suddenly a few drops of rain splattered on the bikes and the bikers. Just as quickly, the rain stopped. The leader of the pack, who had traversed the Mojave many times, thought it might be just a ghost rain, so-called when most of the drops evaporate before reaching the ground. The rain, however, came back, only more of it and harder. The bikers scanned the heavens and saw that bruised clouds had plumped up and were turning dark-er. This was no ghost rain. The riders pulled over to the shoulder and scrambled into rain suits just in time. A hard and steady rain descended on the desert. With no shelter in sight, the bikers continued their journey.

They came to tiny Amboy and the sanctuary of a gas pump overhang at Roy's Cafe. Once a rowdy desert town that went 24-hours a day without missing a beat during the heyday years of Route 66, Amboy began to shrivel in 1972 when Interstate 40 came along ten miles to the north. The town became just a pit stop between Palm Springs and Las Vegas.

Roy's Motel and Cafe, Amboy

The bikers departed between downpours. They passed Amboy Crater, an extinct volcano, and glided along the slick highway running through a valley flanked by the Bullion and Bristol Mountains. Soon they reached what was left of Bagdad.

Once upon a time this was a rip-roaring mining town with a Santa Fe rail depot, a post office, a bustling Fred Harvey restaurant, shops, tourist cabins, and saloons filled with thirsty miners, railroaders, and trav-elers. Now all that remains is a forlorn tree, a railroad siding, pieces of broken glass, and the forgotten graves of Chinese railroad workers who perished during a cholera epidemic.

The slow death of Bagdad started long ago as the mines played out. When the interstate highway was built in the early 1970s and bypassed long stretches of Route 66, the demise of Bagdad — like other stranded towns — was complete. The cult motion picture entitled "The Bagdad Cafe" was not even filmed in Bagdad, but down the highway in Newberry Springs. But once there had been a Bagdad Cafe in Bagdad and it was well known as the only spot for miles around with a dance floor and jukebox. More than one traveler with an overheated radiator ate a meal at the original Bagdad Cafe.

Thoughts of the defunct cafe reminded the bikers that it had been hours since their Needles breakfast. As they saddled up after investigating the remains of Bagdad, the smell of rain — called "Desert B.O." by locals — wafted through the air. The bikers rode through the light rain, all minds were set on a hot meal at the new Bagdad Cafe about forty-five miles ahead in Newberry Springs. By the time the group reached Ludlow, the rain had picked up again and within minutes turned into a full-blown downpour.

None too soon, Newberry Springs appeared through the sheets of water. Ironically this town had originally been called Water because it was the first water point for wagon trains west of the Colorado River. Early travelers quenched their parched tongues at a spring flowing beneath the overhanging rocks of the Newberry Mountains and the settlement became a veritable oasis with its stands of alders, willows, and cottonwoods.

Not so on this day. Wet and weary bikers with growling bellies knew they would find dry comfort and warmth in Newberry Springs. They carefully maneuvered their bikes through the puddles and soft earth that otherwise served as the parking lot at the Bagdad Cafe. Inside they shook off their rain gear like a bunch of

soaked hounds and found places to sit while a waitress handed out mugs of coffee.

The road captain recalled when this cozy rain haven was the Sidewinder Cafe. That was long before filmmakers came to town in 1987 and temporarily changed the Sidewinder's name to the "Bagdad Cafe," the title of an offbeat comedy about eccentric characters who find bliss in the high desert. A few owners later the cafe was officially renamed the Bagdad.

Bagdad Cafe, Newberry Springs

The film spawned a short-lived television series but although the "Bagdad Cafe" may not have become a blockbuster in the United States, audiences in Europe and Japan adored it and still do. Many travelers from abroad make sure that one of the major stops on their Route 66 pilgrimage is Newberry Springs and the Bagdad.

This rainy day was no different. The cafe was packed with rain refugees, including a few other bikers, some standard issue American tourists, and a bevy of visitors from France, Germany, and Belgium.

Seated in the catbird's seat at the far end of the dining room where he could take in the whole scene, was an old man with shaggy white hair and beard. He wore a red flannel shirt and his baggy pants were held up with suspenders. His body listed a bit to the right with his elbow on the tabletop, his cocked head leaning against his open palm. He seemed to be studying the room and everyone in it.

Although he could have been straight from central casting, the bikers learned from their waitress and the discrete whispers of other diners that this old man was not some leftover movie extra. He was much better than that.

The elderly gent was Robert Gray, also called General Robert Gray but much better known on Route 66 and far beyond simply as General Bob. For the next hour this wizard of the road entertained, instructed, castigated, cajoled, and charmed everyone present. As the bikers progressed from coffee to buffalo burgers and finally chocolate malts, they also moved their chairs closer and closer until they encircled General Bob. Like other cafe patrons sitting nearby they were held spellbound by the wild tales and outrageous utterances the old man doled out like heaping dollops of cream.

It seems that not only was this man a general but a five-star general and at one time the general of all the armies of the world. His lineage included English, French, and German bloodlines and he put his age at somewhere over the century mark. That made sense if one were to believe everything he claimed to have accomplished, including composing symphonies and designing spacecraft. Along the way General Bob apparently mastered 9,000 languages, helped build the Golden Gate Bridge, served as a senior diplomatic officer, and worked closely with both the FBI and CIA.

During World War II, he not only helped mastermind allied strategy but also took the time to assassinate Adolph Hitler. When he spoke of how he walked from Ireland to Scotland, not a soul in the joint raised the point that such a feat would have required walking on water. Who knows?

After an hour when some other diners started to stir, the bikers discovered that the rain had finally stopped. A hint of sunshine filtered down and the wet motorcycles parked outside glistened like precious gems.

General Bob was also ready to leave. He announced it was time to go to the nearby motel room he called home and feed his pal, a 100-pound Doberman named Prince.

Outside the bikers wiped off the bike seats and shook hands with General Bob. He offered a wink and a nod and waved his hand like a high priest of the open road giving voyagers his blessing.

Back on the highway, cruising in soft sunlight to whatever waited ahead, the bikers noticed that the sky was clear and bright. Within a few more miles, they saw that the road and the surrounding desert appeared to be bone dry.

Maybe it had been a ghost rain after all. Maybe none of what they encountered behind them was really there. Maybe there was no Bagdad Cafe and no General Bob. Perhaps it was all a mirage. ■

King of the World

— MICHAEL WALLIS

Jamie Constantine does not just live large; he lives triple X large. I knew that the first time I laid eyes on him, astride his big Harley touring bike. A veritable mountain of a man, Jamie is a combination sumo wrestler and Sir John Falstaff — the audacious and witty Shakespearean character both huge in size and appetites.

Jamie not only looks big and rides the biggest Harley made, he also thinks big. A success in the food and drink business for almost four decades, he has watched his popular restaurant, Jamie's Pub, in the coastal town of Scituate, Massachusetts, expand to three more locations in the Boston area.

Since 1994, when he first took to the open road on a regular basis, Jamie has owned a dozen Harleys. He figures those bikes have taken him down some 300,000 miles of highway. Although semi-retired Jamie has no plans to slow down. He and his longtime girlfriend and traveling companion, Linda Scott, spend most of every summer cruising America on a Harley. Their favorite road to take is Route 66.

"The Mother Road is the most biker-friendly highway in the whole U.S. of A," Jamie tells anyone who will listen. "Believe me I've done 'em all and Route 66 is the best, bar none!"

Because of Jamie's zest for life, his great hunger for riding the old highway, and his profound love of all things Route 66, I long ago gave him a nickname that I think fits best. To me he is much more than a King of the Road. Jamie is so big, so grand in body, mind, and spirit that the best moniker for him is King of the World. He wears it well.

My wife, Suzanne, and I have had the pleasure of occasionally cruising the Mother Road with the King of the World and his lady. Often we are joined by two other

Arlen "The Guy with the Horns" Strehlow, Jamie Constantine, and Linda Scott

The King of the World (left) enjoys a meal with Linda Scott and Corey Hebert

A few of their favorites include: New Mexican cuisine in Tucumcari at La Cita followed by warm pie at Del's; thick Bagdad Cafe milkshakes in the Mojave Desert; sizzling burgers right off Mildred Barker's grill at the Frontier Cafe in Truxton, Arizona; and Ted Drewes famous frozen custard. Also on the list are enchiladas hotter than fire at Joe & Aggies in Holbrook; memorable meals in the dining room at La Posada in Winslow; blue ribbon steaks in Oklahoma City, Amarillo, and at Rod's in Williams, followed by bowls of ice cream at Twisters; rainbow trout platters at La Fonda in Santa Fe; and banana splits worth dying for at the Route 66 Diner in Albuquerque.

Still, the one meal shared with our foursome of hearty riding companions that we will remember the most was a breakfast we enjoyed one summer morn at Emma Jean's Hollandburger Cafe on Route 66 in Victorville, California.

The six of us on four bikes — with Linda and Suzanne seated behind their mates — pulled out of San Bernardino early enough to beat much of the crush of traffic. We zoomed up Cajon Pass and after reaching Victorville began to hunt in earnest for a place to eat our morning meal. About the same time, we all spied the mint-green building with a sign on a pole out front. It looked promising. Arlen removed his Viking-like headgear and was halfway to the door before the rest of us had parked our bikes.

well-traveled bikers who have become our friends — Arlen and Tom Strehlow, brothers from Milwaukee, the city where Harleys are created. Arlen, also a substantial man in size, is easily recognized in biker circles and along Route 66 since his normal headgear is a helmet mounted with enormous steer horns. Once you have seen "The Guy with the Horns," as Arlen is known, you will never forget him.

Riding America's Main Street with these four seasoned bikers has brought us some high times, especially at the many cafes, greasy spoons, pie palaces, barbecue pits, sandwich shops, diners, chicken ranches, buffets, and steak houses we have visited along the way.

We have dined with this colorful tribe at the most historic and admired eateries on Route 66. At the drop of a biker's helmet Jamie and Linda can recite some of the most memorable dishes consumed.

A host of hummingbirds darting around the feeders hanging outside the cafe made us all feel good and once we were inside the perfume of frying side meats and the big smile the waitress gave us sealed the deal. Without taking a single bite, we knew we had made a good choice.

Most of the stools at the L-shaped lunch counter were taken but we found prime seats around two of the cafe's four tables pushed together. The busy cook gave us a warm howdy and a wave from the open kitchen while we downed a couple pitchers of ice water in a heartbeat. We soon learned he owned the place. His name was Brian Gentry and the friendly waitress was his wife, Shawna. They lived on the property with their two little girls and served breakfast and lunch to high desert residents and Route 66 travelers every day of the week except Sunday.

Brian and Shawna told us the cafe was originally named the Hollandburger Cafe when Bob Holland and his wife opened for business in 1947. The Hollands operated the cafe for many years followed by a half-dozen other owners who tried to make a go of it until 1979 when Brian's mother, Emma Jean Gentry, bought the place. Brian went to work at the cafe when he was thirteen and came aboard fulltime when he turned sixteen.

"We added my Mom's name to the cafe name," Brian told us. "She worked right here up until the time she died in 1996."

We learned that all sorts of folks had dined at Emma Jean's including Roy Rogers, who resided in Victorville until his death. Besides "The King of the Cowboys," the cafe had also fed truckers, traveling salesmen, hitchhiking soldiers and sailors, and, of course, lots and lots of bikers.

Our group was about half way through our omelets and pancakes when another bunch of bikers strolled in and took the other two tables. It was Jimmy Martinais and his wife Chris from Illinois and some of their pals. They had seen our parked bikes and knew wherever The King of the World stopped the food had to be outstanding. Although Jimmy did not say a word, we knew today was his birthday.

The King of the World held forth in his charming way about the delicious meal before us. He also regaled the crowd with lip-smacking descriptions of some of his signature dishes from Massachusetts. He spoke of his chicken corn chowder, shrimp bisque, and, of course, all the seafood anyone could ever handle.

No fresh fish at Emma Jean's, however, just biscuits and gravy, ham steak, hot cakes. And later for lunch, the Gentrys would offer their half-pound burgers or the famous Trucker's Sandwich loaded with roast beef, bacon, Swiss cheese, green chilies, and surrounded by sourdough bread.

Before we left, The King of the World quietly hatched a plan with the Gentrys. As Shawna carried a tall stack of pancakes covered with blazing candles to Jimmy's table, in unison everyone in the cafe burst into "Happy Birthday."

We all hugged and kissed and then our bunch left. As we walked out the door, I heard Brian say that no one who enters the cafe ever leaves a stranger. With Suzanne snug behind me on the bike, I looked at our fellow road warriors firing up their Harleys and I realized we had done more than just consume a meal. We had partaken of a few moments of delicious camaraderie that would sustain us forever. ∎

Recipes from California

— MARIAN CLARK

*N*eedles remains an oasis before tackling desert heat. It has always been a community filled with gas pumps, repair shops, mom-and-pop eateries, and motor-courts-turned motels.

The site of the 1930s Palms Motel gave way in 1991 to the Old Trails Inn where Mrs. Wilde, the owner, served this wonderful cake to her guests.

Potato Cake
OLD TRAILS INN

1 cup shortening
2 cups sugar
3 eggs
1 cup cold mashed potatoes
2 tablespoons cocoa
1 teaspoon cinnamon
2 teaspoons baking soda
2 cups flour
½ cup sour milk

Gassing up at Roy's in Amboy

In a medium-sized mixing bowl whip the shortening and blend in sugar. Combine thoroughly then add eggs and mashed potatoes. Combine dry ingredients and add to egg mixture along with the sour milk. Mix only until blended. Pour batter into two 8-inch cake pans that have been sprayed with nonstick spray. Bake in a preheated 350 degree oven for 30 minutes. Use your favorite frosting or serve warm without frosting. 12 servings

AT THE IDLE SPURS STEAKHOUSE IN BARSTOW bikers will find western decor and enclosed patio dining. The popular restaurant was built in the 1950s as a home but soon evolved into a restaurant that is both comfortable and casual. Idle Spurs is noted for good steaks and friendly service. Here is one of those "eat to ride and ride to eat" stops. Enjoy!

Black Bean Salsa
IDLE SPURS STEAKHOUSE

1 can (15-ounce) black beans, drained and rinsed
1½ cups cooked fresh corn kernels
2 medium tomatoes, cut and diced
1 green bell pepper, cut and diced
½ cup red onion, finely diced
1 to 2 fresh green Serrano or jalapeño peppers, thinly sliced, including seeds
⅓ cup fresh lime juice
⅓ cup extra-virgin olive oil
⅓ cup chopped fresh coriander
1 teaspoon salt
½ teaspoon ground cumin
½ teaspoon pure ground red chili (not chili powder)

or a pinch of cayenne pepper

Combine all ingredients in a large bowl. Mix well. Set aside to let the flavors blend for a few hours until ready to serve. 4½ cups salsa.

These nachos make satisfying appetizers and the spice can be adjusted for personal taste.

Jalapeño and Chicken Nachos

1½ cup cooked, diced chicken breast
12 ounces cream cheese at room temperature
1 jalapeño pepper, seeded and minced
¼ cup finely chopped red onion
3 cloves of garlic, minced
1 teaspoon ground cumin
1 teaspoon chili powder
1½ cups grated Monterey Jack cheese
Salt and freshly ground black pepper to taste
12 medium flour tortillas

Preheat the oven to 375 degrees. Combine all ingredients except the tortillas in a large mixing bowl. Beat until well blended. Taste and season with salt and pepper.

Melt oil in skillet on medium high heat. Brown each tortilla for about 1 minute. Spread 6 of the tortillas with a generous amount of filling. Cover with remaining tortillas. Place on cookie sheets and bake until bubbling, about 5-7 minutes. Cut into wedges and serve as appetizers in a napkin-lined basket. 72 bite-sized nachos.

Lifelong San Bernardino residents Mike and Maria Austin have winning ways with chili! They started competitive cooking on the International Chili Society circuit in 1989 and through their combined efforts have won several championships.

Mike was the International Chili Society Arizona State Champion in 1991, the California State Champion twice, and placed fifth in the World Championship in 1993. Maria has won the Nevada State Championship and placed eleventh in the World's Championship. Both Mike and Maria have a passion for good times, good chili, and good rides, which includes many trips along Route 66!

Mike Austin's Bun Burner Chili Shack

5 pounds tri-tip or top sirloin, cut into small cubes
1 large sweet onion, finely chopped (about 1 cup)
6 cloves garlic, finely chopped
4 cans (14½ ounces each) chicken broth
1 can (15 ounce) tomato sauce
10 tablespoons pure California chili powder
6 tablespoons ground cumin
3 tablespoons extra-hot New Mexico chili powder
1 tablespoon pasilla chili powder
2 teaspoons garlic powder
Salt to taste

In a large nonstick skillet, cook meat over medium heat one pound at a time, removing meat and setting aside when it is no longer pink. Meanwhile, in a large chili pot, combine all remaining ingredients and simmer for 1 hour. Add meat to sauce and cook for 2 more hours, keeping covered as much as possible. If you want hotter chili, add more New Mexico chili powder.
    10 servings.

Near Goffs

Rancho Cucamonga was once home to Thomas Winery, the oldest winery in California, established in 1839. It was the second winery in the United States. The location is now part of a shopping center at Foothill and Vineyard. To toast the city and the California wine industry, try this champagne punch.

Champagne Punch
Rancho Cucamonga

2 bottles of champagne or Asti Spumante (750 ml each)
1 cup cream de cassis (black currant liquor)
28 ounces of carbonated water

Combine ingredients and serve in 4-ounce stemmed glasses. 22 four-ounce servings.

For decades, AMA Gypsy Tours were a mainstay of the Association's road-riding program, bringing together thousands of enthusiasts every year. But Gypsy Tours disappeared in the late 50s. On their seventieth anniversary year, Gypsy Tours were reinstated and have continued every year since.

> " *G*ypsy Tour time is the great annual get-together of the boys and girls who believe that a motorcycle, the open road, and a meeting point in a shady grove on the banks of a stream or lake are the finest combination in the world."
> (from the American Motorcyclist and Bicyclist Magazine, April 1926)

Make your own gypsy magic today; ride back in time and experience some old magic for yourselves. Ride to eat and eat to ride! Here's one suggested menu. Add your own favorites.

Assorted Appetizers, Snacks, and Sandwiches
Ham, Tomato and Olive Pasta Salad
Southern Baked Beans
Fruit Plate of Watermelon, Cantaloupe, Peaches, and Grapes
French Rolls Garlic Butter
Rich Chocolate Brownies

Spicy Hot Dogs

1 jar (12-ounce) chili sauce
1 jar (9-ounce) grape jelly
3 tablespoons lemon juice
1 pound small cocktail hot dogs

Bring chili sauce, jelly, and lemon juice to a boil. Add hot dogs and heat slowly for 10 minutes. Serve in a slow cooker or chafing dish to keep warm.

California Cheese and Turkey Melt

2 tablespoons low-fat mayonnaise
4 teaspoons basil pesto
8 thin slices sourdough bread
8 ounces sliced cooked turkey breast
4 ounces thinly sliced provolone or mozzarella cheese
8 thin slices tomato

Combine mayonnaise and pesto. Spread 1 tablespoon mixture on each of 4 bread slices. Top each with 2 ounces of turkey, 1 ounce of cheese, and 2 tomato slices. Top with remaining bread slices. Coat a grill or skillet with non-stick cooking spray. Heat to medium. Cook 2-3 minutes on each side until bread is golden. 4 sandwiches.

Ham, Tomato, and Olive Pasta Salad

1 pound penne or other short pasta
¼ cup olive oil, divided
3 garlic cloves, thinly sliced
2 cups (about ⅔ pound) cherry tomatoes, halved
½ cup slivered country ham
1 teaspoon dried oregano
¼ teaspoon red pepper
¼ cup pitted black olives, sliced in half
¼ cup chopped fresh parsley
¼ cup grated Parmesan cheese
Salt to taste
Extra cheese for garnish

In a large pot of boiling water, cook the pasta according to package directions. Drain. Pour 1 tablespoon of the olive oil over the pasta and stir to prevent sticking. Meanwhile, in a large skillet, heat remaining olive oil over medium heat and add garlic. Cook until golden, about 2 minutes. Add tomatoes, ham, oregano, and red pepper. Cook over low heat for about 3 minutes. Pour over the pasta and add olives, parsley, salt, and Parmesan cheese. Toss to combine. Serve in a large salad bowl and garnish with more cheese. May be served warm or cold. 6 servings.

Southern Baked Beans

2 pounds navy beans (small white beans)
Water to cover
1 cup ham, finely chopped
1 small green pepper, minced
1 small onion, chopped
2 teaspoons dry mustard
¼ cup molasses
½ cup firmly packed dark brown sugar
1½ cups catsup
Salt and pepper to taste

Clean and soak beans in water overnight. Rinse and replace water again to cover. Add remaining ingredients and bring to boil. Remove beans to a large baking dish. Cover and place in a preheated 250 degree oven for 7-8 hours. Check several times and add more liquid if necessary. 10 servings.

If you choose to serve burgers or hot dogs at your gypsy picnic, this salsa once served at *Don Salsa*, in Claremont, would make a wonderful addition.

Special Salsa Fresca

(Try this on burgers or steaks and you'll never use catsup again!)
Don Salsa

3 chopped fresh tomatoes
1 chopped fresh onion
3 cloves crushed fresh garlic
1 minced yellow chili, seeded
2 teaspoons chopped fresh cilantro
½ cup tomato juice
Salt and pepper to taste

Combine all ingredients and serve with tortilla chips. Keeps 3-4 days in the refrigerator. For best results, chill tomato juice before adding to salsa. 1½ cups salsa.

For those who want sandwiches, this is the way chicken salad sandwiches are made at Fair Oaks Pharmacy in Pasadena.

Fair Oaks Chicken Salad Sandwiches

2 cups coarsely chopped chicken breast
½ cup thinly sliced celery
½ cup chopped green peppers
½ cup chopped yellow peppers
1 teaspoon Mrs. Dash
½ teaspoon seasoning salt
½ cup mayonnaise

Combine all and mix thoroughly. Serve as salad or sandwich filling. 4-5 servings.

Top the evening off with a daiquiri like this one.

Perfect 66 Daiquiris

Fresh fruit of choice (strawberries, bananas, peaches, or any other)
1 (6-ounce) can of frozen lime-ade concentrate, thawed
Equal amount of rum
Ice

Place enough fruit in food processor or blender to fill 2/3 full. Pour lime-aid concentrate and an equal amount of rum into the blender. Fill blender with ice and turn on machine. Process until smooth.

BARBECUE HAS LONG BEEN A STAPLE IN THE AREA and Pacific seafood is famous world wide so these two traditions have found a perfect home at Rusty's Surf Ranch. Owners Russell Barnard and Mitch Cohen are enthusiastic supporters of both Route 66 and bikers.

Wrapped Salmon
RUSTY'S SURF RANCH

1 8-ounce salmon fillet
1 tablespoon white wine
1 teaspoon butter
Dash of lemon juice
½ medium carrot
¼ bell pepper
¼ cup green or yellow squash
¼ cup chopped tomato
1 teaspoon fresh basil
Dash of black pepper

Santa Monica Pier

Santa Monica Pier, the historic unofficial western terminus of Route 66, has been a magnet for visitors since it first opened in 1909. Perfect for watching sunsets, the pier is also a gathering place for those who crave the sand and sea. The 1922 Looff Carousel with forty-four prancing hand-carved steeds is the sprite-like center of this year-round playground. Don't forget the Ferris wheel that offers an unparalleled view for people watchers and those who love the beach.

One of the many Pier stops that delights visitors year round is Rusty's Surf Ranch, found next to the famous carousel. Often called "the ultimate beach hangout," Rusty's is a full-service restaurant offering lunch and dinner daily, drinks, live entertainment, and dancing. This must-see attraction features a large life-like mural, museum quality displays of vintage surfboards, a great gift shop, historic photos of the Pier, and such eclectic items as Pamela Anderson Lee's Baywatch swimsuit. (The television series was often filmed on the beach nearby.)

Thunder Roadhouse

When it opened in West Hollywood in 1993, Thunder Roadhouse was billed as "America's first motorcycle-theme restaurant." Just as the 60s generation has moved on, so has the roadhouse, but neither are forgotten. For just a while it was the ultimate stop to celebrate freedom of the open road like no other stop: Easy Rider ran nonstop, Captain America Classic Burgers and Kick-Ass Chili were always on the menu, waitresses wore T-shirts inscribed, "Ride to Eat/Live to ride," and patrons could mount motorcycle seats at the bar. Celebrity investors included iron-horse riders Peter Fonda, Dennis Hopper, and Dwight Yoakum. An art nouveau Indian on a bike met patrons at the door and the main dining room featured a teal 1932 Harley VL. In the showroom, bike prices ranged from $12,000 to $30,000. Those choosing to eat on the patio deck were positioned to gaze at more hogs or do some people watching along Sunset Strip. The layout also included a parts shop, vintage bike collection, and clothing boutique. As stars streak across the night sky and disappear, this icon achieved fame then quickly faded, to be remembered by each and every patron who enjoyed a brief but memorable stop.

Julienne the carrot, bell pepper, and squash. Cut a 12x12-inch sheet of heavy duty aluminum foil. Place the salmon at the center of the foil and cover with other ingredients. Fold the foil in half over the combined ingredients and starting at one end, fold over the foil onto itself to form a tight seal. Continue this all the way around until a tight pouch is made. Preheat oven to 375 degrees. Place foil on a cookie sheet or flat pan and bake for 12 to 14 minutes. Open at the table and enjoy the aroma before eating. 1 large or 2 smaller servings.

JUST A FEW BLOCKS TO THE NORTH of Santa Monica Pier, where Santa Monica Boulevard touches Ocean Avenue, is a small stone, set in the grass beneath tall palms. The inscription is memorable. ∎

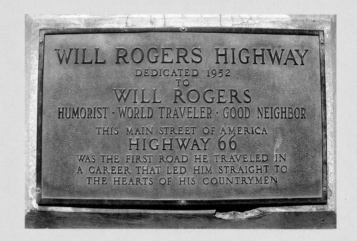

Road Warriors

— MICHAEL WALLIS

Route 66 and everything it stands for remains one of my passions. My study in Tulsa is within easy striking range of the Mother Road of the Joads and "Pretty Boy" Floyd. Chunks of vintage pavement are in a collection of totems that keep me from harm's way. Memories of the places, but more importantly the road warriors — particularly my biker pals — are indelibly stamped in my mind.

These guardians of the old highway know that from Illinois to California the Route 66 revival continues, grows larger, and gains momentum. A monument to wander lust, the highway attracts dedicated enthusiasts who make regular pilgrimages down this road they still consider a genuine celebrity. They have become a family intent on preserving, collecting, and honoring fragments of the past. They gather at annual events along stretches of America's Main Street to strut their stuff on gleaming Harleys, or in Chevys, Fords, and other vintage makes and models that were in vogue when Route 66 was the only way to go. For these road warriors, it still is.

Route 66 has evolved into a venerable and varicose veteran. It is a timeless monument to those who live and work on its shoulders and to the road warriors who prefer its well-worn lanes. ■

171

Hog Handbook

Biker Speak

Garnered from a variety of sources

Anchors — Brakes.

Apes or Ape Hangers — Especially high handlebars, usually found on "choppers" (see below), that force riders to adopt an ape-like posture.

Back Door — The last and hopefully the most experienced rider in a group.

Back Warmer — Passenger.

Bacon — Scabs on biker's body, also called road rash.

Bail — To jump off a bike to avoid a crash.

Bar Hopper — A bike that is not comfortable on long rides.

Beater — A backup motorcycle that owners of expensive cycles use for commuting and errands.

Big Twins — Engines in the larger Harley-Davidson motorcycles.

Black Ice — A biker's worst enemy in winter, this is ice that cannot be seen on the surface of the road.

Blockhead — Harley-Davidson's fourth generation overhead valve Big Twin, introduced in 1984. Sometimes called the Evolution, or shortened to Evo.

Boots — Tires.

Brain Bucket — Another name for a motorcycle helmet.

Bring home a Christmas tree — when a bike leaves the road and crashes into brush, leaving branches and leaves on the bike and biker.

Bro — Short for brother, as in brother of the road.

Buddy Pegs — Footpegs for motorcycle passengers.

Burnout — A maneuver sometimes used by show-off bikers, in which the rider holds the front brake while racing the throttle, causing the back wheel to spin and billow smoke.

Cage — Biker name for cars, the sworn foe of bikers.

Cager — Automobile driver.

Carving — Term for hard, fast cornering on roads with lots of curves and bends.

Catwalk — Riding a cycle on the rear wheel only, often referred to as a "wheelie."

Chopper — Custom motorcycles with all the superfluous parts "chopped" off, or modified, to make the bike faster.

Coupon — A traffic or speeding ticket.

Crotch Rocket — A sportbike designed for optimum speed.

Dresser — A cycle set up for long-distance touring.

Fairing — A plastic shroud that deflects rain and wind from the rider.

Fat Boy — Introduced in 1990, this model — which features solid wheels, both front and rear — is the pinnacle of the Softail custom family of Harley-Davidson motorcycles.

Fathead — Slang name for Harley-Davidson's Twin Cam 88 engine introduced in 1999.

Flathead — Harleys manufactured from 1930-1948 with valves moved to the opposite sides of combustion chamber for more power

Flower Pot — Name for an inexpensive helmet.

Flying Low — Speeding.

Free Lunch — Bugs in your mouth and teeth.

Foot Padding — When a novice rider "walks" his or her cycle around at low speeds.

Garbage Wagon - A derogatory term used by outlaw bikers to describe fancy touring bikes.

Hack — Name for the sidecars, or small carriages for passengers attached to the side of a motorcycle.

Harley Wrench — A hammer.

Hog — Common nickname for a Harley-Davidson motorcycle.

H.O.G. — Harley Owners Group, founded in 1983 and the world's largest factory-sponsored motorcycle organization with 1,000 H.O.G. chapters and more than 400,000 members around the globe.

Hydroplane — What occurs when the motorcycle tires start to float on top of water on the road, causing them to lose contact with the surface.

Knucklehead — Harley-Davidson's first overhead-valve Big Twin, introduced in 1936. Legend has it the name comes from the valve covers that look like the knuckles of a clinched fist.

Lane Splitting — Sometimes called "white-lining," this is when a biker rides between lanes of traffic on a freeway.

Mill — Engine.

Milwaukee Tractor — Name of endearment for a Harley.

Motor — Term used by motorcycle cops to describe their bike.

One Percenter — Outlaw bikers or outcasts who choose to follow their own rules and beliefs. Less than one percent of the population fits this category.

Organ Donor — A helmetless biker, sometimes referred to as a metal head.

Panhead — Harley-Davidson's second-generation overhead-valve Big Twin, introduced in 1948. Old-timers claim the name is from valve covers, which resemble small roasting pans.

Rice Burner — Pejorative name for any motorcycle manufactured in Japan.

Road Rash — Marks on biker's body as result of bike going down on the pavement.

RUB — Rich urban biker, a derisive term often used by seasoned Harley riders when referring to doctors, lawyers, and other professionals (a.k.a. "yuppie scum") who purchase expensive motorcycles as status symbols.

Scoot or Scooter — Slang name for a motorcycle.

Shovelhead — Harley-Davidson's third generation overhead-valve Big Twin, introduced in 1966. The name comes from the head that resembles a coal shovel.

Skid Lid — Name for a motorcycle helmet.

Sissy Bar — A backrest attached behind the passenger's portion of the saddle.

Springer — A popular Harley cycle with springer forks, exposed springs to lessen the impact on rough roads.

SQUID — Squirrelly Young Kid with no business being on a bike.

Streetfighter — Also known as a "hooligan" cycle, this is a sportbike stripped of all superfluous bodywork.

Sturgis — A small town in South Dakota that annually hosts the most famous of all biker rallies.

Twisties — A road with many twists and curves.

Two Up — Term used when a passenger rides on the back of the motorcycle.

Willie G. — Grandson of the founder of Harley-Davidson, Willie G. Davidson serves as styling vice president and has achieved national celebrity status as the driving force behind the firm's phenomenal success.

Biker Mother Road Essentials

Garnered from a variety of sources

Open Mind	Flat repair kit
Helmet	Spare fuses
Eye protection	Rain suit
Bottle(s) of drinking water	Toolkit
Jacket	Dealer list
Boots	Tire pressure gauge
Gloves	Flashlight
Identification	Ear plugs
Set of Route 66 maps	Sunscreen
Insurance papers	Steering lock
Spare bike key	AMA and/or HOG Membership card
Bungee cords	First aid kit
Cargo net	Totes
Cleaner and rag	

Tip: Bring plenty of bandanas or do-rags. Also known as "cowboy air conditioners," bandanas thoroughly soaked in ice water and tied around neck or head make for a cooler ride.

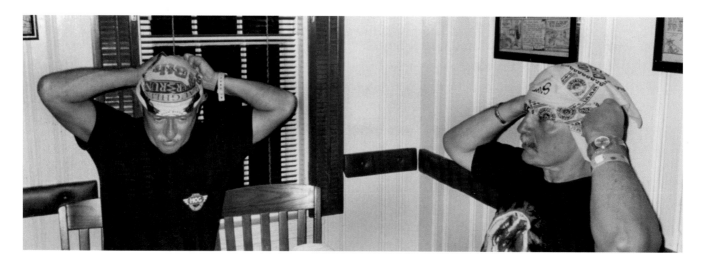

Biker Pit Stops

A list of authorized Harley-Davidson dealers located on the Mother Road in the eight Route 66 states

ILLINOIS

Illinois Harley-Davidson
1301 S. Harlem Avenue
Berwyn, Illinois 60402
(708) 788-1300
(877) 464-1450

Chuck's Harley-Davidson
2027 Ireland Grove Road
Bloomington, Illinois 61704
(309) 662-1648

Chicago Harley-Davidson
6868 N. Western Avenue
Chicago, Illinois 60645
(773) 338-6868

Chicago Harley-Davidson Downtown
68 E. Ohio Street
Chicago, Illinois 60611
(312) 274-9666

Chicago Harley-Davidson
520 N. Michigan Avenue
Ste. 324
Chicago, Illinois 60611
(#12) 755-9520

Conrad's Harley-Davidson
1541 Riverboat Center Drive
Joliet, Illinois 60431
(815) 725-2000

Hall's Harley-Davidson, Inc.
3755 N. Dirksen Parkway
Springfield, Illinois 62707
(217) 528-8356

MISSOURI

Cycle Connection Harley-Davidson
I-44 Exit 6
5014 Hearnes Blvd.
Joplin, Missouri 64804
(417) 623-1054

Doc's Harley-Davidson Motorcycle
Sales & Service
930 S. Kirkwood Road
Kirkwood, Missouri 63122
(314) 965-0166
(866) 333-DOCS

Ozark Harley-Davidson, Inc.
2300 Industrial Drive
Lebanon, Missouri 65536
(417) 532-2900

Gateway to the West
Harley-Davidson
3600 LeMay Ferry Road
St. Louis, Missouri 63125
(314) 845-9900

Widman Harley-Davidson
3628 S. Broadway
St. Louis, Missouri 63118
(314) 771-7100
(800) 404-6880

Denney's Harley-Davidson of
Springfield
3980 W. Sunshine Street
Springfield, Missouri 65807
(417) 882-0100

Bourbeuse Valley Harley-Davidson
1418 Highway AT (Exit 247)
Villa Ridge, Missouri 63089
(636) 742-2707

KANSAS

None on Route 66. Closest dealer
is in Joplin, Missouri

OKLAHOMA

Myers-Duren Harley-Davidson of Tulsa
4848 S. Peoria Avenue
Tulsa, Oklahoma 74105
(918) 743-4440

Route 66 Harley-Davidson
3637 S. Memorial Drive,
(Hwy.51 & Memorial Dr. Exit)
Tulsa, Oklahoma 74145
(918) 622-1340

Harley-Davidson World Shop
3433 S. Broadway
Edmond, Oklahoma 73013
(405) 478-4024

Harley-Davidson World
2823 S. Agnew Avenue
Oklahoma City, Oklahoma 73108
(405) 631-8680

TEXAS

Tripp's Harley-Davidson, Inc.
6040 I-40 West
Amarillo, Texas 79106
(806) 352-2021

NEW MEXICO

Chick's Harley-Davidson
5000 Alameda Boulevard N.E.
Albuquerque, New Mexico 87113
(505) 856-1600

Santa Fe Harley-Davidson
3501 Cerrillos Road
Santa Fe, New Mexico 87507
(505) 471-3808

ARIZONA

Grand Canyon Harley-Davidson
I-40 Exit 185 (10 miles west of
    Flagstaff)
Bellemont, Arizona 86015
(928) 774-3896 (866) 867-4243

Mother Road Harley-Davidson
2501 Beverly Avenue
Kingman, Arizona 86401
(928) 757-1166

CALIFORNIA

Harley-Davidson of Victorville, Inc.
14522 Valley Center drive
Victorville, California 92392
(760) 951-1119

Quaid Harley-Davidson
25160 Redlands Boulevard
Loma Linda, California 92345
(909) 786-8399

Bartel's Harley-Davidson
4141 Lincoln Boulevard
Marina del Rey, California 90292
(310) 823-1112

Biker Mother Road Test

Gleaned from a variety or sources and old scooter tramps

Answer yes to most of the statements on this list and chances are you are a true Route 66 Biker Road Warrior.

If only the back of your hands are sunburned

If you have spent at least one night at the Blue Swallow Motel in Tucumcari, New Mexico, or the Munger Moss Motel in Lebanon. Missouri

If you believe "helmet hair" is a fashion statement

If you carry more photographs of your bike than your kids

If you always warn others about the speed trap waiting at Arcadia, Oklahoma

If you register for wedding gifts at a bike shop or Mother Road curio store

If most of your tee shirts are emblazoned with motorcycles or Route 66 shields

If you know who Tod and Buz were and forgive them for not riding bikes

If you have either a child or a pet named Harley

If you think of sushi as bait and eat chicken fried steak for breakfast side meat

If you can identify insects by their taste

If your favorite periodicals are *American Road*, *Route 66 Magazine* and *HOG Tales*

If you have enjoyed a handcrafted sandwich at Wrink's Market in Lebanon, Missouri, or at Eisler's Brothers Store in Riverton, Kansas

If you have had your hair cut or been shaved by Angel Delgadillo

If you have ridden the twisties leading up to Oatman in the dark

If you own any artwork by Bob Waldmire or Jerry McClanahan

If you have acquired larger saddlebags for your bike to carry your Route 66 kitsch

If you believe that even a rainy ride on the Mother Road means it's a good day

If you know all the words to "Get Your Kicks" (extra credit if it is on your telephone answering machine)

A "yes!" from Michael Wallis

If your personal library is primarily books about bikes and roads

If your heroes are Willy G. and Cyrus Avery

If you celebrate both the anniversary of Route 66 (November 11) and the date you got your bike

If your bike has ever been parked in front of the Old Curiosity Shop in Erick, Oklahoma

If you have even considered trying to eat the Big Texan 72-ounce steak (extra credit for successfully eating it)

If it takes you the better part of a day to ride the 13.2 miles of Mother Road in Kansas

If you have dined on calf fries at the Hammet House in Claremore, Oklahoma

If you have ever hunted for the "Spook Light" (extra credit for spotting it)

If you have competed in a butt darts tournament (extra credit for winning)

If you have visited the Pine Breeze Inn near Bellemont, Arizona

If you ever stayed in the Elvis Suite at the Tradewinds Motel in Clinton, Oklahoma

If your favorite three-piece suit is chaps, leather vest, and leather jacket

If you ever slept in a Wigwam at Holbrook, Arizona

If you do most of your Christmas shopping at your local Harley dealer and Teepee Curios in Tucumcari

If you have ever had a conversation with General Bob Gray at the Bagdad Cafe in Newberry Springs, California

If your favorite sports hero of all time is Andy Payne

If your best footwear has steel toes

If you have seen the film version of "The Grapes of Wrath" and "Easy Rider" more than three times (extra credit for being able to recite entire lines from the films)

If your bike has at least one Route 66 decal

If you cannot remember the last time you ate at a chain fast-food joint

If you have stood on "the" corner in Winslow, Arizona

If you have ever had Sunday dinner at the Ariston Cafe in Litchfield, Illinois

If you know the exact site location of the extinct Regal Reptile Ranch

If you own any underwear imprinted with either Route 66 shields or motorcycles

If you have attended both a John Steinbeck Awards Banquet and a Route 66 HOG rally

If you know the definition of devil's rope

If you possess a nugget of petrified wood, a wooden nickel from the Round barn at Arcadia, Oklahoma, and any souvenir from Exotic World at Helendale, California

Biker Celebs

Peter Fonda	Lindsay Wagner	Dwight D. Eisenhower	George Orwell
Dennis Hopper	James Dean	Laurence Fishburne	Che Guevara
Elvis Presley	Roy Rogers	Sam Elliot	Arnold Schwarzenegger
Dwight Yoakum	Malcolm Forbes	King George VI	Sammy Davis, Jr.
Jackson Browne	Charles Lindbergh	Steve McQueen	Dan Aykroyd
Sammy Hagar	Flip Wilson	Clark Gable	Mickey Rourke
Jay Leno	Ann Richards	King Hussein of Jordan	Franklin Graham
Larry Hagman	Marlon Brando	Bob Dylan	Reba McIntyre
Robert Blake	George Bernard Shaw	Keenan Wynn	Wynona Judd
Billy Idol	Lauren Hutton	Sir Ralph Richardson	Queen Latifa
Lorenzo Lamas	Gary Bussey	Howard Hughes	Georgia O'Keeffe

Flip Wilson on Route 66

Biker Tunes For The Mother Road

Most good road songs make good biker tunes and vice versa. Bear in mind that motorcycles always have been entwined with the mythology of rock n' roll. Unquestionably the unofficial Biker National Anthem remains "Born to Be Wild," by Steppenwolf. Listed below is a selection of songs to get your motor running.

"Route 66," any version will do, but especially Asleep at the Wheel

"Born To Be Wild," "Magic Carpet Ride," Steppenwolf

"Take It Easy," or just about any song from The Eagles

"The Ballad of Easy Rider," The Byrds

"Roll Me Away," "Against the Wind," or, just about any song from Bob Seger

"Midnight Rider," The Allman Brothers

"Born To Run," Bruce Springsteen

"Leader of the Pack," The Shangri-Las or Melissa Etheridge

"Harley," Kathy Mattea

"Unknown Legend," Neil Young

"Lost Highway," Hank Williams

"Live and Die in L.A.," Wang Chung

"On the Road Again," Willie Nelson

"Let it Roll," Bachman-Turner Overdrive

"Road House Blues," The Doors

"Kings of the Highway," Chris Isaak

"City of the Angels," Journey

"Back in the U.S.A.," Edgar Winter

"Endless Highway," Bob Dylan

"Fun, Fun, Fun," The Beach Boys

"King of the Road," Roger Miller

"Miles of Texas," Asleep at the Wheel

"Rockin' down the Highway," The Doobie Brothers

"Two Lane Highway," Pure Prairie League

"Land of Enchantment," Michael Martin Murphey

"Hitch a Ride," Boston

"The Last Trip to Tulsa," Neil Young

"Happy Trails," Roy Rogers and Dale Evans

"Oklahoma," Rogers and Hammerstein

Food Festival Fun on Route 66

TASTE OF CHICAGO — THE BIGGEST SUMMER FESTIVAL IN CHICAGO
When: 10 days surrounding the 4th of July each year
Grant Park (where Route 66 begins).

HORSERADISH FESTIVAL — COLLINSVILLE, ILLINOIS
When: First weekend in June each year, Woodland Park
Food booths, entertainment, family fun, and horseradish games.

WORLD'S LARGEST CALF FRY FESTIVAL AND COOK-OFF — VINITA, OKLAHOMA
When: 2nd Saturday every September
Cowboy games, plenty of country food, crafts, and over 2,000 pounds of calf fries.

FRIED ONION BURGER FESTIVAL — EL RENO, OKLAHOMA
When: 1st Saturday each May
Celebrating onion burgers that have been prepared in El Reno since early in the 1900s. The "big burger" prepared at the most recent festival weighed over 850 pounds. Includes a car show, food, crafts, and children's activities.

PINTO BEAN FESTIVAL — MORIARTY, NEW MEXICO
When: 2nd Saturday each October, City Park
A pinto bean cook-off, arts and crafts booths, food vendors, classic cars, farmer's market, bands, a parade, rodeo, and carnival.

NEW MEXICO WINE FESTIVAL — BERNALILLO, NEW MEXICO
When: Labor Day weekend
The premier wine-tasting event of the Southwest. Exhibits from New Mexico Wineries, a juried art show, agricultural products showcase, and live entertainment. The American Bus Association has listed this festival as one of the "Top 100 Events" in North America.

GRAPE HARVEST FESTIVAL — RANCHO CUCAMONGA, CALIFORNIA
When: 1st Weekend each October, Epicenter Parking Lot at Rochester
Celebrating the first winery in California, established in 1839 at what is now the corner of Foothill and Vineyard on Route 66.

Route 66 Associations

Route 66 Association of Illinois
2743 Veterans Parkway, Suite 166
Springfield, Illinois 62704
http://www.il66assoc.org

Route 66 Association of Missouri
P.O. Box 8117
St. Louis, Missouri 63156-8117
http://www.missouri66.org

Kansas Historic Route 66 Association
P.O. Box 66
Riverton, Kansas 66770
http://route66.itgo.com/ks66.html

Oklahoma Route 66 Association
P.O. Box 21382
Oklahoma City, Oklahoma 73156
http://www.oklahomaroute66.com

Old Route 66 Association of Texas
P.O. Box 66
McLean, Texas 79057
http://www.mockturtlepress.com/texas/

New Mexico Route 66 Association
1415 Central NE
Albuquerque, New Mexico 87106
http://www.rt66nm.org

Historic Route 66 Association of Arizona
P.O. Box 66
Kingman, Arizona 86402
http://www.azrt66.com

California Historic Route 66 Association
1024 Bonita Avenue
LaVerne, California 91750
http://www.wemweb.com/chr66a.html

Canadian Route 66 Association
P.O. Box 31061
#8-2929 St. Johns Street
Port Moody, British Columbia
Canada V3H 4T4
www.homepage.mac.com/route66kicks/Route66/

Belgium Route 66 Association
www.historic66.com

Norwegian Route 66 Association
5238 Radel
Norway
www.route66.no

California Route 66 Preservation Foundation
P.O. Box 29006
Phelan, CA 92329-0066
www.cart66pf.org

National Historic Route 66 Federation
"Working Nationwide to save the legendary highway."
P.O. Box 1848
Lake Arrowhead, CA 92352-1848
http://www.national66.com

Index of the Road

Index of Recipes

About the Authors

Michael Wallis has published 11 books, including the bestseller *Route 66: The Mother Road*. An avid and battle-scarred Harley rider, Michael frequently leads tours down Route 66 for the Harley Owners Group and others.

Marian Clark is the author of best-selling *Route 66 Cookbook, The Main Street of America Cookbook,* and *The Southwest Heritage Cookbook.*